A Beginner's Guide to the OLD TESTAMENT

ROBERT DAVIDSON

SAINT ANDREW PRESS

EDINBURGH

*The Publisher acknowledges
financial assistance from
The Drummond Trust
towards the publication of this volume.*

First published in 1992 by
SAINT ANDREW PRESS
121 George Street, Edinburgh EH2 4YN.

Reprinted 1993

ISBN 0 7152 0637 0

British Library Cataloguing in Publication Data
A catalogue record for this book is available
from the British Library.
ISBN 0-7152-0637-0

Unless otherwise specified, the quotations in this book are taken from the
REVISED ENGLISH BIBLE (REB), copyright © 1989 Oxford University
Press and Cambridge University Press.

The original source for this book was a series of articles published in
Life and Work, the Record of the Church of Scotland.

This book has been set in 11.5/13 pt Garamond.

Printed and bound by
Athenaeum Press Ltd, Newcastle upon Tyne.

Contents

To Ken, Jean and Moyra

Preface

Over the past fifteen years I have contributed to the Church of Scot
land magazine *Life and Work* several series of articles on various
aspects of the Old Testament. They made no scholarly claims. They
were written solely to provide a 'Beginners' Guide to the Old Testament' for those—and there are many of them in the church—
who are frankly puzzled by the Old Testament, have little real
knowledge of it, but are still curious enough to wonder what it is all
about. These articles sought to provide information and to focus
attention on something of the spiritual value of the Old Testament.
This small volume, which contains in part a selection from these
articles, comes in response to the request of several people who
wished to have the material in more permanent form. For the sake of
consistency all Biblical quotations are now taken from the Revised
English Bible, unless I have thought there are good reasons for
departing from it.

I am grateful to the former editor of *Life and Work*, R D Ker-
nohan, who commissioned the articles, and to the present editor
Peter Macdonald for permission to use the material. The dedication
is an inadequate recognition of the unfailing support and encouragement received from my senior chaplain, Ken Gardner and his
wife, and from my junior chaplain Moyra M'Callum, during my
Moderatorial year.

Robert Davidson 1992

Introduction

I am more and more convinced of two things about the collection of books which we call the Old Testament. The *first* is this. For many people, not least those within the church, the Old Testament, apart from a few familiar, well-loved passages such as Psalm 23, is more or less a closed book, largely unread, very often misunderstood. It is a closed book because in many ways it is difficult and puzzling. Many otherwise highly intelligent people, committed to the Christian faith, will openly admit that they don't know how to handle the Old Testament. If this is where you find yourself, don't despair, don't feel guilty about it. There has seldom been a time in the church's history when the Old Testament has not been something of a problem.

Some people have tried—and some still try—to solve the problem by reading into the Old Testament things which are not really there. We are told, for example, in Genesis 14:14 that Abram gathered together a posse of 318 retainers to pursue certain royal cattle thieves who had swooped in from the east. Why 318? Well, if you turn the number 318 into its equivalent in Greek letters you get the initial letters of the name 'Jesus', and the letter in the Greek alphabet which looks like the sign of the cross. Abram's 318 men are, therefore, a pointer to the salvation won for us by Jesus on the cross. That was the explanation given by an ingenious early Christian writer. It tells you, of course, nothing about the Old Testament passage at all. The writer could have used the same argument if there had been 318 palm trees at Jericho; and so could we if there happened to be 318 applicants for a job. If that is the kind of approach to the Old Testament which appeals to you, then this book is not for you. I suspect most of us would rather remain puzzled than take the above way out.

But *second*, many people are anxious to find something which will help them to open this closed book. When they do open it and begin to learn to read it intelligently and with understanding, they often find it challenging and exciting, strangely relevant to their lives in a way in which—dare I say it—parts of the New Testament are not. So if you are puzzled, but willing to learn, this book is for you. If you have no problems with the Old Testament, you are either very lucky or you are fooling yourself.

The names we give to things are important. Give a dog a bad name, and you know what happens. Perhaps this is one of our problems. We talk about the 'Old Testament.' The very word *old* is unfortunate, particularly when we set it alongside something which we call the New Testament. It suggests that here is a book which is old hat or obsolete, something no longer needed which can have little to say to our rapidly changing world, when what is new today is in danger of being old and outdated tomorrow. Anything the Old Testament once had to say is therefore said better and more clearly in the New Testament. It is worth remembering that the 'Old Testament', as the title of a collection of books, was not an expression ever used by Jesus, nor was it found among the earliest Christians. What we call the Old Testament, usually in its Greek translation, was for the early church simply the Bible, Scripture, the sacred books. It was some time before there was anything called the New Testament to place alongside it. This was the Scripture which spoke to the church of the same God who had come into the world in Jesus.

But these are also the books, particularly in their Hebrew form, which continue to be the authoritative Scriptures of the Jewish community, the Bible which has enabled the community to survive across centuries of wandering and persecution. We must be prepared to take this fact seriously as Christians. You do not need to be a Christian to understand these books. To claim that there is only one way to understand them, the Christian way, is spiritual arrogance. The 'Old Testament' is no more than a Christian label—and I sometimes think an unfortunate one—attached to books which continue to speak about God and the purpose of living, to people who find it impossible to accept the Christian claims.

There is, indeed, a sense in which the Old Testament does not need the New Testament nearly as much as the New Testament needs the Old. I find it impossible to understand Jesus or the message of the New Testament apart from its roots in the Old: but I can understand how what we call the Old Testament can in its own right, apart from the New Testament, be the basis of a vital faith. That is why I think it is wrong for Christians to think of the Old Testament as *merely* preparation for the New. That was a mistake that Christians began to make quite early in the history of the church. The Old Testament tended to be regarded as important because it provided proof texts for the coming of Jesus and the mission of the church. To view it in this way, however, is inevitably to be very selective in the passages to which we pay attention. So we fasten on, for example, to Isaiah 7:14, very dubiously translated following the Greek translation, as 'A virgin shall conceive and bear a son', or we turn to Isaiah 9, with its promise of the coming of a child born to rule. Often this means taking passages and using them in a sense quite different from their original meaning. Matthew 2:15 quotes from Hosea 11:1 the words, 'Out of Egypt I have called my son', claiming that the flight of Mary and Joseph with the baby Jesus took place to fulfil what the LORD had declared through the prophet. Yet if you turn to the passage in Hosea 11 from which these words come, you will see that Hosea is referring to something that happened some 500 years before his own day. He is recalling the story of the Exodus, the deliverance of the enslaved Hebrew people from Egyptian oppression. The son of whom the passage speaks is Israel. Hosea is certainly not thinking of an event which was to take place 700 years after his own day.

Now there are very good reasons why Matthew's gospel quotes Old Testament texts in this way. The writer believes that Jesus is the long-expected Jewish Messiah, the final and true revelation of the God to whom the Old Testament bears witness. The only way he could convince his fellow Jews of the truth of this, was to quote texts from the Jewish scriptures. Any good Jewish Rabbi or teacher would have understood what he was doing, even if he did not accept Matthew's conclusions. But if this is all we are going to do with the Old Testament, then we are not going to understand the word of God contained within its pages. If we take only passages which we think lead us on into the New Testament, we shall miss the rich variety of insights and the challenge which the Old Testament as a whole can bring us. Don't go to the Old Testament simply looking for Jesus. Let it speak to you in its own terms and in its own words. Don't think of it first of all as the *Old* Testament. Don't hang any label round its neck. Try to listen to it.

As soon as we try to listen, however, we come up against difficulties, which we must take seriously. We find ourselves transported into a strange world, a world in many respects light years away from our world of computers, pop music and jeans, a world which knows nothing of many of the problems of our modern industrial and technological society, no long-term unemployment, no threat of a nuclear holocaust. Look at family relationships and you find yourself in a society in which there is nothing wrong in a man having more than one wife, providing he can afford them; a society in which a man is legally obliged to marry his widowed sister-in-law if she has been left childless. This should remind us that here is a collection of books that come to us from the world of the Ancient Near East, a very different world from our European or Americanised world, different even from the world of the Middle East today. You may pay a visit to Israel or Jordan today, but that won't take you into the world of the Old Testament except in a very superficial way. When you meet a Jew in Jerusalem today, don't think that he is like the Jew who lived in Jerusalem under King Solomon. He probably has more in common with his cousin who still lives in New York. Nor should we make the mistake of assuming that the modern state of Israel is in some sense the Israel you meet in the Old Testament. It isn't.

All this means that we must be prepared to use our imagination, and the knowledge we possess, to take a journey back in time, and into a world which does not share many of the ideas and the things we take for granted. It will do us no harm if, on the journey, we take with us some guide books to help us find our way. So in turn, we shall try to familiarise ourselves with the land out of which the books of the Old Testament come, the people whose experience is recorded in them, the way in which the books come to be in their present form, the faith to which they bear witness, and what that faith has to say to us today. For me, for many years, it has been a worthwhile journey. I hope it will be equally worthwhile for you.

1

A Hitch-Hiker's Guide to the Land

There is no need to tell a Scot about the importance of his 'ain country.' In Vancouver or Dunedin, India or South Africa, wherever Scots have gone, the sound of the pipes and drums, the songs of the Isles, the country dancing, bring a lump to the throat. Back the memory goes, often somewhat romantically, to that north-east fishing community, or the Eildon Hills, or Glasgow. The land, in which people are born and brought up, has a lasting influence upon them. The size and shape of the land often has a profound and decisive influence upon the history of the people who live in it. It has been claimed that you can't understand the Russians as people unless you remember the long winter nights, and the snow and ice which grip much of the land for months on end: that, and the vast expanse of the Russian landscape into which you can fit the whole of the USA, Canada and Mexico. It is the same landscape, and these same harsh winters, which have decisively influenced the history of Russia, as both Napoleon and Hitler found out to their cost.

The Old Testament comes to us out of the experience of a people who, for over a thousand years before the time of Jesus, settled in a land once known as Canaan. In extent it is more or less the same as the land now occupied by the modern state of Israel, including the West Bank. That land has left its indelible mark both upon the people and their history. Here there are no endless plains or vast distances to cover. It is a small country, how small we seldom stop to remember. Big events don't need a big setting. Its natural boundary on the West is the Mediterranean Sea, and on the East the Jordan Valley. From West to East is, on average, roughly the distance from Glasgow to Edinburgh. From its traditional northern frontier in what is now southern Lebanon, down to the southern desert which separates it from Egypt, is roughly the distance from Glasgow to Inverness. Although it is small, it is, like Scotland, a land of dramatic contrast. From West to East it divides naturally into three regions.

THE COASTAL PLAIN

With an extensive coastline on the Mediterranean Sea you might have expected the people of this land to have been natural sea-farers. They weren't. The coast is mainly shifting sand dunes with few breaks to provide a natural harbour. It is further to the north where the coastline is more broken, in what is now Lebanon, that we find in ancient times the Phoenicians, the great sea-traders and explorers. Apart from those who fished the inland lakes, along the line of the Jordan valley, the Hebrews were land-lubbers. Remember Jonah? It was sheer desperation to escape from God that made him take to sea with a one-way ticket for a Mediterranean voyage. Not that it did him much good! When the Hebrew people enjoyed a brief period of imperial greatness in the tenth century BC, King Solomon decided to use the sea to develop his export-import trade. The home base for his fleet, however, was not on the Mediterranean, but in the far south at Ezion Geber on the Gulf of Akaba, an arm of the Red Sea. The demand for 'experienced seamen', to provide the officer corps for his fleet, had to be met by his northern ally, King Hiram of Tyre (1 Kings 9:26). The call of the sea was not heard in many Hebrew families.

The sandy shore of this coastal plain was broken at its northern end by the Carmel mountain ridge which rises steeply from the Mediterranean and cuts its way inland. The main towns in the plain were not on the coast—sea side resorts were not yet in vogue. They were situated inland, back from the coast, along the line of the main trade route, 'the way of the sea' which ran north from Egypt along the coastal plain. At the Carmel ridge, the route cuts inland through the pass of Megiddo out onto the plain of Jezreel, then north through Galilee to Damascus and beyond. Many a fierce battle was fought for control of the strategic pass of Megiddo. The name 'Armageddon', which is used, *eg* in the book of Revelation (Revelation 16:16) as the scene of the final conflict between God and all those who oppose his purposes, is simply a corruption of Hebrew for 'the hill of Megiddo.'

THE CENTRAL HIGHLANDS

As we move inland from the coastal plain, we come to the central hill country. In the far north, beyond the fertile plain of Jezreel which extends to the Mediterranean near modern Haifa, are the hills of Galilee rising to over 3000 feet and dominated on the northern horizon by Mount Hermon, over 9000 feet above sea level and often snow-capped. Travelling south we move across the plain of Jezreel to the hill country of Ephraim, patterned by many a valley and deep ravine, particularly on the eastern slopes. Along the watershed of the hills ran, from north to south, the central communication system, little more than a rough track. At points where this intersected with valleys running east and west stood some of the most important early settlements, such as Shechem, and later Samaria, capital of the northern kingdom of Israel when the united kingdom of David and Solomon divided. The uplands continue south into the hills of Judah which cradle Jerusalem. Their eastern slopes dip sharply into the Jordan valley, particularly near the Dead Sea. Further south the hills fall away into the rolling countryside of the Negeb and on into the desert dividing Canaan from Egypt.

THE JORDAN VALLEY

The natural geographical eastern boundary of the land is marked by the rift valley of the Jordan. The River Jordan rises in the slopes of Mount Hermon, descends quickly into Lake Huleh, then flows along the Huleh valley, carving for itself an ever deepening channel until by the time it flows into the Sea—or rather Lake—of Galilee it is over 600 feet below sea level. From the Lake of Galilee it winds its way south until it disappears into the 'sea of salt', the Dead Sea—again, a large Lake. At this point it is 1200 feet below sea level, with the bed of the Dead Sea at its southern end a further 1300 feet below sea level—the lowest point on the surface of the earth.

To move down from the hills into the valley of the Jordan is to enter a world of shimmering, stifling heat, and, wherever there is sufficient water, an area of lush tropical vegetation, particularly in the lower Jordan valley. In Old Testament times this was the haunt of marauding lions who came 'from Jordan's dense thickets' (Jeremiah 49:19) to attack the flocks on the pasture lands. Although the Jordan marks the natural geographical boundary of the land, it is not an effective political or military barrier, being at points little more than a muddy burn. Beyond the Jordan stretches a high plateau, home of the Edomites, the Moabites and the Ammonites. Along this plateau ran another of the main north-south trade routes, 'the king's highway' (Numbers 20:17). It was along this route that some of the Hebrews who had been slaves in Egypt attempted to move north out of the desert, before cutting across the Jordan opposite Jericho, to enter what for them was their promised land.

This then is the land of Canaan. In it people had settled for centuries before the coming of the Hebrews. We can trace signs of settled life, for example, in Jericho back to around 7000 BC. It was a hospitable land; on the whole a fertile land, with areas of rich soil that supported a thriving agricultural economy, 'a good land, a land with streams, springs, and underground waters gushing out in valley and hill, a land with wheat and barley, vines, fig trees and pomegranites, a land with olive oil and honey' (Deuteronomy 8:8). This attractive scenario, however, depended upon one essential precondition—*rain*. The rains normally come in winter, brought by the westerly winds blowing in from the Mediterranean. They begin in late October or early November. By the end of March the hot dry winds blow in from the eastern deserts. The lush pasture and the carpets of flowers begin to wither: the landscape becomes parched. The book of Deuteronomy correctly notes one of the main differences between this land and the land of Egypt.

The land which you are about to enter and occupy is not like the land of Egypt from which you have come, where, after sowing

4

your seed, you regulated the water by means of your foot as in a vegetable garden. But the land into which you are about to cross to occupy it is a land of mountains and valleys watered by the rain of heaven.

(Deuteronomy 11:10-11).

If irrigation was hard work in Egypt, at least it ensured a dependable supply of water based on the annual rise and fall of the Nile. But if the rains failed in Canaan, drought and famine were a grim reality and many people found themselves taking the road down to Egypt in search of food (see *eg* Genesis 12:1ff).

The need to ensure the coming of the life-giving rain is one of the central themes of the religion of the peoples who were there in the land before the Hebrews arrived on the scene. They worshipped gods and goddesses of fertility and celebrated their victory over the powers of death and drought. It was a religion which, in the form of the worship of Baal, was to have a lasting attraction to the Hebrews when they settled down to till the soil.

The land of Canaan had another and different problem. Its position guaranteed that it was destined to have an uncertain and stormy political history. This small land was a bridge between the great imperial powers of the ancient Near East. To the south was Egypt, to the north and east the civilisations of the Mesopotamian valley, the empires of Assyrian and Babylon. Apart from a brief period in the tenth century BC under the united monarchy of David and Solomon, the land was at the mercy of powerful foreign invaders. Armies, as well as traders, marched along 'the way of the sea' and struck inland. Politics were often dominated by the need to decide whether to back Egypt against Assyria or vice versa, or whether to join with other small surrounding states in the ancient equivalent of NATO, and fight for independence from 'big brother', in whatever shape big brother might appear. Small may be beautiful: but its smallness, combined with its geographical position, guaranteed that for the land out of which the Old Testament came, there could only be a stormy history.

2

The People
and their History

Tucked away in the back of our minds, most of us have an 'identik-it' picture of a Jew, the kind of Jew we would have expected to meet in ancient Israel. It covers certain physical features, the colour of the skin, the shape of the nose. It also carries the image of someone who belongs to a people racially pure and deeply religious, if not indeed fanatical in defence of their faith. It is a picture which hardly squares with what we find in the Old Testament about the people of Israel. When we ask 'who were the people of Israel?' and 'when did their history begin?', we seem to be asking simple questions. There are, however, no simple answers. Many scholars today believe that it does not make sense to talk about Israel as a people in the Old Testament until we come down to the time of the establishment of the kingdom of David and Solomon in the tenth century BC. Only then is there a recognisable state with a central government and a clear identity. This Israel, however, did preserve stories about its past. Although the outlines of this past become more and more blurred the further we go back into the mists of antiquity, there are certain things which I believe we can say with reasonable confidence.

THE RACIAL MELTING POT

The prophet Ezekiel, in one of his biting attacks on the people of Jerusalem in his own day, says:

> Canaan is the land of your ancestry and your birthplace; your father was an Amorite, your mother a Hittite.
>
> (Ezekiel 16:3)

The Amorites, 'the people of the west', is a general name given to the people who had settled in the region which now comprises Israel, Lebanon and Syria. Like the word 'European' today, it covers people of different origin and background. The Hittites were conquerors who had come down into the area from the north. This 'land of Israel's ancestry' had experienced many an invasion and contained settlements of people from many different places before even the Hebrews came on the scene. If Canaan was geographically a bridge between the great civilisations of the ancient Near East, there had been heavy traffic on the bridge before the pilgrim forefathers of the Hebrews take the stage.

Let us take a glimpse at this melting pot as we see it through the eyes of some Egyptian documents. Around the middle of the fifteenth century BC, the Egyptian Pharaoh Thut-mose III attempted to stabilise Egyptian control over Canaan in a series of military campaigns. There is a communiqué in which he celebrates his victory over an alliance of Canaanite kings in the region of Megiddo. Defeats, of course, were never noted unless they could be passed off as victories. Certain things never change! The communiqué lists the names of well over one hundred cities, most of them in the coastal plain of Canaan, or in the valley of Jezreel and to the north. We are not talking about cities in our modern sense, such as Edinburgh or Glasgow or even Perth, but they were settlements, centres of population worth noting in a military communiqué. The landscape of Canaan, particularly in certain areas, was dotted with such settlements.

It is also in Egyptian documents from about this time that we find increasing references to the activities in Canaan of people known as the *habiru* or *hapiru*. They are obviously a disruptive element in the political scene. Correspondence flows back and forward between the Egyptian authorities and some of their vassal kings in Canaan, as these kings plead for help from the Egyptians against the *habiru*, or vehemently deny that they are in league with the *habiru*. These *habiru* do not seem to belong to a particular race. They appear rather as guerrilla groups or outlaws, lacking any rights in settled society. They may well be refugees who have been forced to leave their own communities for social or political reasons. We cannot simply identify the first Hebrews in the Old Testament with these *habiru*, but it is probably in just such a period of political unrest and instability that the first elements of what later became the people of Israel began to infiltrate into the land of Canaan. The word 'Hebrew', in fact, in early Old Testament narratives, is most frequently found on the lips of Egyptians or Philistines, and carries with it the kind of contempt that people often convey when they use the word 'foreigner.'

THE PILGRIM FOREFATHERS

The book of Joshua describes the beginnings of the people of Israel in the following way:

> Long ago your forefathers, including Terah the father of Abraham and Nahor, lived beyond the Euphrates and served other gods. I took your ancestor Abraham from beside the Euphrates and led him through the length and breadth of Canaan. I gave him many descendants ....
>
> (Joshua 24:2-4)

This passage, and several other Old Testament passages (*eg* Genesis 11:27ff) point to the beginnings of the people of Israel as lying outside Canaan with a group who travelled westwards from somewhere in the Mesopotamian valley. When Abraham, who is regarded as the pilgrim forefather of the people, took this westward road with his family, he was doing what many other groups had done before, often as the result of pressure from other groups spilling into the Mesopotamian valley from the desert or from the north. The nature of the stories about Abraham we shall discuss later (see pp 44ff). Canaan, however, had no difficulty in assimilating another migrant group. The central highlands were on the whole sparsely populated, and it is along the central highlands that Abraham and his family first moved with their flocks. As far as possible they seem to have avoided direct contact or conflict with the main centres of

8

population. The quarrels which they had, both among themselves and with the locals, were quarrels about grazing rights (Genesis 13:6-8) and about access to watering facilities for their flocks (Genesis 26:16-22). To such a small group of migrants, Israel traced her beginnings. Indeed the clans which later were thought of as making up the people of Israel were said to be 'the sons of Jacob', grandson of Abraham. It was Jacob who, according to two traditions in Genesis (Genesis 32:27-28 and 35:9-11) was renamed 'Israel' and gave his name to the people.

Many stories were preserved that told how this people was related to other tribal groups in the area, particularly the tribes who occupied the land on the other side of the Jordan, the Moabites, the Ammonites (Genesis 19:36-38) and the Edomites (Genesis 36). They are all said to trace their roots back to the family group of Abraham.

SETTLING DOWN

The precise steps which led this migrant group to the point where it became the dominant and controlling element in the land of Canaan, are far from clear. It must have taken hundreds of years. It was certainly less tidy than is suggested by a casual reading of the books of Joshua and Judges. It seems clear, however, that a decisive factor in the march to nationhood was the coming from across the Jordan of a group who had experienced slavery in Egypt. They brought with them a dynamic faith in a God who had delivered them from Egypt. Liberation theology was on their lips. This God who had set them on the path to freedom was the God who had met them at a mountain in the desert. They had been set free to be the people of this God and to worship only this one God. This faith was to become the rallying cry under which different Hebrew clans would unite in face of a common enemy (see *eg* Judges 5). Everything, however, points to the fact that when the common threat receded, people went back to their crofts and indulged in bitter inter-clan rivalry. They had their equivalent of the Clan Macdonald and the Campbells. There they settled down to cultivate their own cabbage patch and to learn from their Canaanite neighbours not only how to farm successfully, but also how to worship the local gods and goddesses who gave fertility to the soils and guaranteed good harvests.

The book of Deuteronomy demands that the inhabitants of Canaan who were in the land before the Hebrews came, should be exterminated and that under no circumstances should there be any intermarriage with them, in case it led to religious disloyalty (Deuteronomy 7:1-6; 20:15-18). That was not what happened. Indeed, Deuteronomy looks very much as if it is trying to close the stable door after the horse has bolted! The old population remained, side by side with the Hebrews. There was social contact. There was intermarriage. The man who came to be regarded as the model king of his people, David, had, according to the book of Ruth, a Moabite great granny; and his son and successor, Solomon, was the fruit of his union with the wife of a Hittite soldier!

THE NONCONFORMIST MINORITY

In religion it was prudent to make the best of both worlds. Few Hebrews seem to have had any difficulty in combining belief in the God who had brought them out of Egypt with the worship of the local gods and goddesses. It made sense to hedge your bets and to have as many friendly powers on your side as possible. Those who believed that they should only worship one God, the LORD who had brought the people out of enslavement in Egypt, were always in the minority and always fighting an uphill battle for most of the Old Testament period. Yet it was this stubborn minority who ensured that in the fulness of time there would come the literature which we now call the Old Testament, and that, while the names of most of the other peoples who settled in Canaan are important only to scholars, we still sing the hymns of ancient Israel.

The picture we get in the book of Judges and in the early chapters of Samuel is that of a somewhat close-knit federation of clans, prepared to express, when need arose, a common loyalty, but otherwise lacking any real loyalty and without any central authority or government. That might have lasted long enough had it not been for one new factor, which led the clans to put their foot on the path which took them to the nation state of Israel, a nation powerful enough to be treated, for a while, with respect by other nations, a nation which grasped at power and almost lost its soul.

Nothing more unites a family than an interfering outsider. In the case of the Hebrew families who settled in Canaan, that interfering outsider was the Philistine. They were part of a wave of 'sea peoples' who came from across the Mediterranean to try to settle on the north African coast, in Egypt, and then in what is now Israel and Lebanon. Early in the twelfth century BC, one group of these sea peoples, repulsed by Pharaoh Rameses III from gaining a foothold in Egypt itself, settled on the coastal plain of Canaan. They were to give us the name by which, until recently, the whole land was known—Palestine, Philistine land. Well-organised into a close knit federation of five major cities, and with a well-equipped army, they began to expand inland into the central highlands. Conflict with the Hebrews was inevitable. A series of Philistine victories, including the capture of the Hebrews' most sacred religious symbol, 'the ark', the sign of the LORD's presence in the midst of his people (1 Samuel 4), faced the Hebrews with a stark choice—unite or perish. Some more permanent and cohesive political structure, which would cut across old and often divisive clan loyalties, was needed. It was found by adopting a long-established form of government in the ancient Near East—kingship.

The first king, accepted after initial hesitations, was Saul. His reign was brief and he receives a bad press in 1 Samuel, which is concerned to show why and how royal power passed from Saul to David. In spite of initial successes against the Philistines, Saul is depicted as a man suffering from serious psychological disorders, a man who underestimated the importance of the religious lobby represented by Samuel, a man jealous of the new local hero, his son-in-law, David. No wonder he was jealous, when he heard the words of one of the pop songs of the day:

> Saul struck down thousands,
>> but David tens of thousands.

(1 Samuel 18:7)

When the Philistines pushed in strength along the plain of Jezreel, Saul faced them at Mount Gilboa. There he died, together with his son Jonathan, and the elite of the army. Their tragic fate is immortalised in the Old Testament equivalent of the Scottish folk song 'The flowers of the forest are a' wede awa', in a lament attributed to David:

> Israel, upon your heights your beauty lies slain!
>> How are the warriors fallen!

> Beloved and lovely were Saul and Jonathan;
>> neither in life nor in death were they parted.
>> They were swifter than eagles, stronger than lions.

(2 Samuel 1:19,23)

For the moment it must have seemed that this new style kingship was no more politically effective than the old, loose-knit clan loyalties it was designed to replace. This was to reckon without one of the most fascinating and towering figures in Hebrew history.

Most of us have a fairly romantic picture of *David*. There is David the shepherd boy, probably composing some of his more familiar psalms, *eg* 'the LORD is my shepherd', while he tended his flock on the hillside near his home town of Bethlehem. There is David, the young hero of Israel, slaying the Philistine champion Goliath with a pebble from his sling (if you want an interesting 'whodunnit', compare 1 Samuel 17 with 2 Samuel 21:19 and 1 Chronicles 20:5). The reality is somewhat different and more interesting. David was a tough cookie. He had to be. For months he was on the run from Saul, little more than a guerrilla leader of a band of social misfits and desperados. When things became too hot for him in his own country, he was not averse to signing on as a mercenary in the service of the Philistines. Yet all the while he was forging the weapon which took him to the throne and kept him there, the nucleus of a professional army which would owe loyalty to no one but himself (see 1 Samuel· 19-27). David was shrewd, with ever the eye for the main chance. He was prepared to use anyone and everything to get what he wanted. He used his time in the Philistine army to provide himself with a base from which, through military forays and diplomatic marriages, he became the favourite son of the southern tribes of Judah. There, in the south, by popular acclaim he became king at Hebron for over seven years, while the northern clans remained loyal to a surviving son of Saul. David played his cards patiently and skillfully till disaffection in the north brought a delegation of elders from the north to Hebron to offer David the loyalty of the northern clans.

It is a measure of David's political astuteness that he realised that if he were to rule successfully over a united kingdom, something had to be done to break down rivalry and suspicion between north and south. His solution was Jerusalem. He captured this Jebusite city situated on the bridge land between north and south and transformed it into the capital of his newly united kingdom. It was the Washington of ancient Israel. Unlike Saul, he did not make the mistake of underestimating the importance of the religious factor in the life of his people. To Jerusalem he brought the ark, visible symbol of the presence of the LORD, to be there at the centre of the nation's life (2 Samuel 6). Soon he was effectively using the power his new status gave him. The army, capably led by his ruthless, down-to-earth commander Joab, dealt with the Philistines. David was on his way to controlling an empire which was to include not only the land of Canaan, but most of present day Jordan, Syria and Lebanon.

David's years in Jerusalem are vividly sketched in 2 Samuel 9-20 and in the opening chapters of 1 Kings:

— the cold blooded murder of one of his own soldiers, Uriah the Hittite, to give respectability to his passion for Uriah's wife, Bathsheba (2 Samuel 11-12);
— family problems, culminating in a revolt led by Absolam his son, a revolt which came within an ace of succeeding (2 Samuel 13-18);
— continuing undercurrents of tension between north and south which led to an attempted secession movement by disaffected northern elements (2 Samuel 20);
— the bitter struggle to secure the succession to the throne between his sons Adonijah and Solomon, as the old king lay dying (1 Kings 1-2).

No other narratives in the Old Testament are so full of human interest, so crowded with cameos of fascinating characters.

What should the verdict on David be? In a sense he was lucky. He came to the fore at a time when there was something of a power vacuum in the ancient Near East, once the Philistines had been dealt with. Egypt was in decline; the new imperialist power from the east, Assyria, had not yet occupied the stage. But let nothing detract from his greatness. He took the fragmented clans and wielded them, temporarily at least, into a nation. Out of a defeated people he created an empire. Ruthless he could be, yet he evoked intense loyalty from those around him, a loyalty no more finely expressed than in the words of one of his mercenaries who, when David's fortunes were at a low ebb, refused to transfer his loyalty to Absolam: 'As the LORD lives, your life upon it, wherever you may be whether for life or death, I, your servant, shall be there' (2 Samuel 15:21).

Solomon's accession to the throne was marked by a blood bath in which he liquidated his rivals, including Joab, David's old commander-in-chief, who had backed the wrong horse in the accession stakes. Unlike David, Solomon had not come up the hard way. He had been born with a silver spoon in his mouth, and during his lifetime the silver turned to gold. Jerusalem became an important cultural and commercial centre: but there was a price to be paid.

The civil service developed apace. The country was divided into twelve administrative districts, each under a regional governor, and each responsible for providing for one month in the year the not inconsiderable quantities of food and provisions for the royal household (1 Kings 4). Taxation was heavy. There was investment in public works. Extensive building operations went on throughout the land, not least in Jerusalem. The city of David was given a substantial facelift. The first temple to the LORD within the city was built on Mount Zion, and in it was housed the Ark. The significance of the temple and the hopes surrounding it, are well expressed in Psalm 132:

... the LORD has chosen Zion, desired her for his home:
'This is my resting place for ever;
here I shall make my home, for that is what I want.'

(Psalm 132:13-14)

The temple was built according to native Canaanite specifications, designed and executed by craftsmen from Tyre. Although it was an impressive building, some 100 feet long by 35 feet wide, it was small compared with the palace complex nearby which Solomon built for himself.

Such public works made heavy demands on labour. According to 1 Kings 5:13, 'King Solomon raised a forced levy from the whole of Israel amounting to thirty thousand men.' (Other passages suggest that Solomon used only 'aliens' for this purpose, eg 2 Chronicles 2:17) No doubt some of his fellow countrymen, as they spent one month in three sweating it out in the logging camps in Lebanon or in the stone quarries, had their own views on the new glory that was Solomon's. Although many passages speak of the lavish wealth which flowed into Jerusalem through trade and treaties, it was not enough to satisfy his expensive tastes, including a harem of 700 wives and 300 concubines. Solomon accumulated a substantial budget deficit. Hiram of Tyre, his northern ally, was prepared apparently to give him almost unlimited credit. We hear, however,

15

of Solomon having to pay for some of his building activities by ceding to Hiram, 'twenty towns in Galilee', not that Hiram thought very much of the towns! (1 Kings 9:10-13)

There were ominous signs that the empire David had founded was not destined to last. In the north, in and around Damascus, and in the south in Edom, independent régimes arose, with Solomon seemingly powerless, or not sufficiently interested, to bring them to heel (1 Kings 11:14-25). One of his own officers in charge of labour gangs in the north, Jeroboam, was involved in a plot to set up a northern secession movement. It was nipped in the bud. Jeroboam, however, found political asylum in Egypt, whence he returned after Solomon's death to play a leading role in the establishment of an independent northern kingdom. Much is made in the Old Testament of Solomon's reputation for wisdom, and many proverbs are attributed to him; it is doubtful, however, whether in his dealings with his own people, he had a fraction of the wisdom of David.

The transformation from the old tribal federation to the state and empire of David and Solomon took place within a period of less than a hundred years in the tenth century BC. It brought with it ideas which, for good and for ill, were to live on and influence the thoughts and the destiny of people for many centuries. We cannot understand the Old Testament unless we are steeped in the traditions abut the royal family of David, Jerusalem the city of God, and the temple of the LORD in that city.

A PEOPLE DIVIDED

If a few days can be a lifetime in politics, so can a few years in the history of a people. Anyone living in Jerusalem in the heyday of Solomon, around 930 BC, might well have wondered if he had strayed into a totally different world some ten years later. The Empire of David and Solomon collapsed almost as quickly as it had arisen. Both David and Solomon ruled over a people who were at heart still two nations, north and south. Solomon did little to draw them more closely together. While he lavished money and energy on making

Jerusalem a capital worthy of imperial greatness, the north seems to have become increasingly impoverished. Perhaps Solomon did not understand the two nations, no more than some people in the affluent south understand the economic problems of the north in Britain today. Certainly his son and successor, Rehoboam, did not. The flashpoint came when Rehoboam went north to Shechem to be acclaimed as king there. In spite of wise advice from some of his elder statesmen, he refused to listen to reasonable requests from the north for a lightening of the harsh treatment they had received. Rehoboam was not for turning; he promised them more of the same:

My father made your yoke heavy, but I shall make it heavier. My father whipped you, but I shall flay you.

(1 Kings 12:14)

The north seceded. Jeroboam, one of Solomon's former directors of labour, returned from exile in Egypt to be its first king. For the next two hundred years there were two kingdoms, the larger economically more prosperous and politically more influential northern kingdom of *Israel*, with its capital eventually in Samaria, and the smaller southern kingdom of *Judah*, centred on Jerusalem, a kingdom which remained loyal to the royal house of David.

When you read the history of these two kingdoms in 1 Kings 13ff—and perhaps it is not the most popular reading from the Old Testament—it is important to remember that you are reading an account of events as seen through the eyes of men who lived in the south. There is a strong southern bias. The writers believed that right from the beginning the northern kingdom of Israel was illegitimate, schismatic, and heretical. The true faith was preserved only in Jerusalem; the sole legitimate, divinely sanctioned royal family was the family of David. An account of the same period written by someone from the north would have read very differently; as different as an account of Scotland today, written by a home based Scot and active member of the Scottish National Party, would be from one written by an Oxbridge trained civil servant, who had spent all his working days in and around London. Not only so, but it is impossible on the basis of the material in Kings and the parallel narratives in Chronicles to write a satisfactory history of the divided kingdom. The information is not there. Again and again we are told that if we want further information we should go and consult the official state archives. Unfortunately these archives have not survived. What we *are* given is a religious commentary on the divided kingdoms, a commentary which seeks to show how disobedience to the word of the LORD and divided religious loyalties lead to disaster. Politically north and south were often at each other's throats. They fought over disputed territory north of Jerusalem. They sometimes tried to use other neighbouring countries to weaken each other. They are uncertain as to the best policy to pursue to come to terms with the ever increasing menace of the threatening giant from the east, Assyria.

ISRAEL

Let's begin by taking a brief look at the northern kingdom of Israel. It was to last for two hundred years. Lacking any established and generally acceptable royal family, its internal political stability was fragile. On several occasions during its comparatively brief history, an army commander engineered a palace *coup d'état* and seized power (see *eg* 1 Kings 16:15ff). Furthermore it had a religious problem. Jeroboam realised from the outset that, if he were to retain the loyalty of the people, something had to be done to counter the religious mystique of Jerusalem. So he inaugurated religious festivals in the north to rival those celebrated in Jerusalem. He sought to increase the prestige of two ancient religious sites in his territory, one in the south at Bethel, the other in the north at Dan. There he placed his gold bull calves. The writers of Kings regard them with horror, but it is doubtful whether Jeroboam thought he was doing anything novel or wrong: 'You have gone up to Jerusalem long enough,' he said to his people, 'here is your God, Israel, who brought you up from Egypt' (1 Kings 12:28).

The bull, symbol of fertility in Canaan, was probably thought of as no more than the pedestal on which stood the invisible God of Israel. It is the northern answer to the Ark, the throne of the invisible God in Jerusalem.

Israel had its problems, but it prospered economically, even if the prosperity was patchy, with society becoming increasingly polarised between rich and poor, the exploiters and the exploited. Against such a society some of the prophets, like Amos, thundered in vain (see pp 56ff). Standing astride the main trade routes of the ancient Near East—it controlled the pass of Megiddo—Israel carefully cultivated relationships with surrounding countries, and cemented these relationships in the usual diplomatic way—by royal weddings. Increasing foreign influence and the growth of royal power provoked a backlash from certain traditional prophetic movements, as we see in the stories about Elijah and Elisha in 1 Kings 17ff.

One apparently trivial incident is revealing. You can read about it in 1 Kings 21. King Ahab had plans to extend his palace gardens. Nearby was a vineyard, worked by a small-time peasant farmer called Naboth. Ahab makes Naboth a reasonable offer—a better vineyard in exchange, or, if he prefers, the fair market price. Naboth refuses. The vineyard, he claims, is not his to give. It is family property which he holds in trust, to hand on to the next generation. King Ahab is enough of an Israelite to know that he is up against a brick wall. He cannot ride roughshod over traditions of his people, traditions which have the sanction of religion behind them. But he is upset; he takes to his bed and sulks. Enter his wife Jezebel, a dynamic woman who would grace any episode of 'Dallas' and would certainly have been a match for J.R. Brought up outside Israel, she is accustomed to royalty getting what it wants. How can the king be thwarted by an insignificant peasant farmer? Who calls the shots in Israel? If Ahab is too lily-livered to take what he wants, she will get it for him. She takes steps to have Naboth liquidated with due semblance of legality. There's your vineyard, she says to Ahab, take it! But in the very act of going down to take it, Ahab comes faces to face with the prophet Elijah who tells him in no uncertain terms, 'you have sold yourself to do what is wrong in the eyes of the LORD' (1 Kings

19

21:20). Elijah is no warm hearted humanist standing up for human rights. He can be just as ruthless as Jezebel. What he is doing is querying the assumption that royal power is absolute. King, as well as commoner, in Israel must be subject to a higher law, the law of the LORD. He is insisting that the nation and the royal family exist to serve the will and purposes of God. If they don't, there can only be one outcome—disaster. Disaster for Israel was to come in the shape of the Assyrians who in the year 721 BC captured and destroyed Samaria. The northern Kingdom, with most of its population deported and scattered, lapsed into obscurity as a province of the Assyrian empire.

JUDAH

The southern kingdom of Judah lasted for nearly another 140 years. It survived the Assyrian onslaught, which sealed the fate of Israel, by the skin of its teeth. Heavy tribute had to be paid, as one by one the small Judean towns fell into the hands of the Assyrians (2 Kings 18:13ff). The book of Kings, however, also preserves the story of how the LORD miraculously intervened at the eleventh hour to destroy an Assyrian army besieging Jerusalem (2 Kings 19:35ff). This undoubtedly must have served to increase 'the guid conceit' that the southern kingdom had of itself. What had happened in the north could never happen to Judah. They were God's people in a way these northerners had never been. They held two trump cards:

(a) *The temple at Jerusalem.* This was not merely a national shrine; it was the very dwelling place of God. The LORD had chosen this to be his earthly home. God, the LORD of hosts, the God who controlled the destiny of all nations, was in their midst. Therefore neither city nor temple could ever be destroyed. In confidence they sang their hymns:

God is in her midst; she will not be overthrown,
    and at the break of day he will help her.
Nations are in tumult, kingdoms overturned;
    while he thunders, the earth melts.

> The LORD of Hosts is with us;
>> the God of Jacob is our fortress.

(Psalm 46:5-7)

> See, the kings assemble; they advance together.
> They look, and are astounded; filled with alarm they panic.
> Trembling has seized them there; they toss in pain like a woman
>> in labour,
> like the ships of Tarshish when an east wind wrecks them.
> What we had heard we saw now with our own eyes
>> in the city of the LORD of Hosts, in the city of our God;
>>> God will establish it for evermore.

(Psalm 48:4-8)

When in the year 587 BC the Babylonian armies were hammering at the gates of Jerusalem, people were prepared to resist to the death, confident in the faith that God would never let his temple and city be destroyed.

(b) *The royal family of David.* The family of David gave a measure of internal political stability to Judah. There were no army-led *coup d'états* as in Israel. This had its religious roots in the belief that the family of David stood in a special relationship with God. Such a relationship guaranteed that there would always be a descendant of David on the throne in Jerusalem. Psalm 132 puts it this way:

> The LORD swore this oath to David,
>> an oath which he will not break:
> 'A prince of your own line I will set on your throne.
> If your sons keep my covenant
>> and heed the teaching that I give them,
> their sons in turn for all time will occupy your throne.'

(Psalm 132:11-12)

It is small wonder that amid the many ups and downs of life, a mood of self-confidence remained in Jerusalem right to the bitter end.

There were many prophets in the city to keep on saying to the people, 'All is well, all is well, God will protect us.' If there were an odd-ball prophet, such as Jeremiah, saying something different, he could always be dismissed as a heretic and a scaremonger.

But the end did come in 587 BC at the hands of the Babylonians. The temple was reduced to a smoking ruin; the then king of the family of David carried off into exile. With this, the need to think again became urgent. The dream of national power and glory had gone, perhaps for ever. The confident, optimistic religious mood of the people had been shattered. Some of what they had believed to be God's promises had turned out to be false. As many of the people of Judah went off into exile, or tried to survive in their devastated homeland, they had to face a future, stripped of much of what they had considered essential to their faith. That is never easy; but it can lead to a new faith, built on a more lasting foundation.

AFTER EXILE

'Keep right on to the end of the road' was one of Sir Harry Lauder's favourite songs. But what happens when you believe you have reached the end of the road, and it has turned out to be a dead end as far as faith is concerned? That was the mood of many Jews who went into exile to Babylon when Jerusalem was destroyed in 587 BC. A prophet of the exile lets us into their thoughts:

> Jacob, why do you complain, and you, Israel, why do you say,
> 'My lot is hidden from the LORD, my cause goes unheeded by my God?'
>
> (Isaiah 40:27)

> But Zion says,
> 'The LORD has forsaken me; my lord has forgotten me.'
>
> (Isaiah 49:14)

When you have lived through tragic days, it is reasonable enough to conclude that either God no longer cares or that he is powerless to do anything to help. The answer the prophet gives is to ask these people to take a fresh look at the great certainties central to their faith, certainties nowhere more finely expressed than in the words:

> Can a woman forget the infant at her breast,
> or a mother the child of her womb?
> But should even these forget, I shall never forget you.
>
> (Isaiah 49:15)

That, God's promise, may be excellent theology, but what does it mean in down to earth terms for a people broken and in exile? There were those who kept holding out to the people the hope that one day there would be a return to Jerusalem and the beginning of a new and better life. That hope was soon to be realised.

RETURNING HOME

The door opened in 539 BC when Cyrus of Persia smashed the power of Babylon and became the new master of the ancient Near East. For the next two hundred years the Jews, and many other peoples, were to live under a Persian régime whose general attitude to its subject peoples has been called one of 'benevolent tolerance.' Provided imperial law and order remained undisturbed, there was little interference in local customs or religious practices. Cyrus himself, in what was probably a shrewd political move, entered Babylon claiming to be the favoured son of the Babylonian gods, sent to restore the material and spiritual well-being of the city. He adopted a similarly enlightened policy towards those who had felt the heavy hand of Babylonian oppression. In his own words:

> The holy cities beyond the Tigris whose sanctuaries had been in ruin over a long period, the gods whose abode is in the midst of them, I returned to their place and housed them in lasting abodes. I gathered all their inhabitants and restored them to their dwellings.

23

What this meant for the Jews in exile in Babylon you will find described in the books of Ezra and Nehemiah. Jews who wished to return home to Jerusalem—and by no means all did so—were given every encouragement to do so. When they returned, inspired by some of the magnificent visions of a new Jerusalem in Isaiah 40-55, they were soon to be disillusioned. They came back to face hard times and a continuing struggle for survival. Morale seems to have been at a low ebb, but thanks to some fairly aggressive prophetic arm twisting (see Haggai), the temple in Jerusalem was rebuilt by 515 BC. This is the building usually referred to as 'the second Temple', Solomon's being the first. The rebuilt temple provided the community with a visible focus for its religious life, but it left many problems still to be tackled.

Leadership came from two men. There was Ezra, 'the scribe', or as the Good News Bible puts it, 'a scholar with a thorough knowledge of the Law which the LORD, the God of Israel, had given to Moses' (Ezra 7:6). His main priority was to lay down the guidelines to help the community to follow its religious vocation. The other key figure was Nehemiah. Acting with some kind of official authority from the Persian authorities, he sought to counteract the continuing low morale of the people. He organised the rebuilding of the city walls to provide security, and tackled some of the serious social and political problems. There is much that we do not know about Jerusalem in the fifth century BC. We are not even sure whether Ezra came before Nehemiah, or Nehemiah before Ezra, or whether they were contemporaries in Jerusalem. Certain important new features of Jewish life, however, were beginning to emerge.

THE NEW COMMUNITY

Although there were still, and always would be, those who dreamed of the restoration of an independent state under a Davidic king, the community in and around Jerusalem was in fact more of a congregation than a nation; a congregation gathered round the restored temple, the worship in which was designed to keep the community in a right relationship with God. This community was well on the way to becoming 'the people of a book.' While earlier a prophet would say, 'Thus says the LORD', and claim that the word he spoke had come to him directly through personal experience, the final authority for a scribe like Ezra was, 'Thus it is written.' We are here at the beginning of the Bible as the authoritative book, controlling the life and faith of a people. In a square just inside the Water Gate, Ezra read to the assembled people from 'the book of the law of Moses, which the LORD had enjoined upon Israel' (Nehemiah 8:1). In all probability that book contained Genesis to Deuteronomy, Torah, God's instruction and teaching, his revelation of himself to Israel (see pp 34ff).

Although Jerusalem was no longer the capital of an independent state, it was on the way to becoming something much more important; the spiritual centre and home of a people who were increasingly scattered across the known world, the *Diaspora*, from a Greek word meaning to disperse. There were Jews who decided to remain in Babylon instead of returning to the homeland: there were Jewish mercenary troops in the service of the Persians in garrison towns such as Elephantine on the southern borders of Egypt: there were Jews settled in Alexandria, one of the great cosmopolitan cities in the ancient world: there were Jews dispersed for a variety of reasons in many lands and many cities. They could hardly be expected to journey to Jerusalem to worship God. To meet their needs there came into being a new religious institution, the synagogue, a local meeting house where Jews could gather to keep their faith alive, by hearing 'the book' being read and expounded, and by joining in prayers. The synagogue was in no sense intended to replace the temple in Jerusalem. Pilgrimage to that temple remained the desire of every godly Jew. Much, however, of what was of lasting importance for Jewish identity and faith now centred on the synagogue. It was the synagogue which became the true bearer of that faith when, after the destruction of the second Temple by the Romans in AD 70, there was no longer any temple in Jerusalem.

One of the most pressing problems facing the post-exilic community—as indeed it faces any religious community—was how to preserve its own distinctive life and faith in the midst of an alien and sometimes hostile world. There were no easy answers. The answer of some people in Jerusalem, illustrated by certain features of the policies of Ezra and Nehemiah, was not only to build a physical wall to provide national security, but to build a spiritual wall to exclude the threatening world outside. They would become 'a holy people' by practising a policy of religious apartheid. The danger in this is of a community turned in upon itself, concerned only with its own salvation. Walls are not much use as bridges. At the other extreme we find the Jewish garrison at Elephantine in southern Egypt, anxious to cultivate good relationships with the people among whom they are living. They are prepared to recognise other gods and goddesses alongside the God of Israel. They build bridges, but the danger here is that they end up having nothing vital or distinctive to offer to the world. How do you strike a balance? If to a large extent under Persian rule the Jews were left to work out their own answers, a new challenge was soon to be on their doorstep.

THE CHALLENGE OF THE WEST

In the year 333 BC Persian power was virtually destroyed by Alexander the Great, son of the king of Macedon in Greece. Alexander was not only a military genius, he was the apostle of a way of life to which we give the name *Hellenism*. Hellenism had its roots in the rich traditions of Greek civilisation, particularly as it had flourished in Athens, its culture, its literature, its thought. It stood for a civilised way of life based on the city state. It brought with it a common universal language, Greek, and regarded those who did not share its values or speak its language as 'barbarians.' Although politically, after Alexander's early death, his empire fragmented—the Jews finding themselves sandwiched between the Seleucid dynasty to the north and the Ptolemies of Egypt in the south—the whole world of the ancient Near East remained deeply influenced by western, Hellenistic, values, values which were fostered by the planting of new cities, often inhabited by Greek army veterans.

Although Hellenism proved in many ways attractive, especially to upper class, educated Jews, it was almost inevitable that, sooner or later, there would come a clash between this Hellenistic claim to cultural superiority with its one world outlook, and the more exclusive attitude of the Jew with his belief that his God was the only God, and his peculiar way of life based on a book the only true way of life. The flashpoint came in 167 BC because of the policy and the megalomania of the Seleucid king, Antiochus IV. He had given himself the grandiose title 'Epiphanes', the manifestation of God; his enemies had another name for him, 'Epimanes', the madman! He made the fatal mistake, which many others had made, of underestimating the importance of the religious factor in Jewish life. Returning from a rather morale-bruising encounter with Roman forces in Egypt, he decided to teach his Jewish subjects a sharp lesson. He desecrated the Jerusalem temple, its treasures making a useful contribution to his war chest. He erected in the temple an altar to Zeus Olympius, the president of the Greek gods—an altar satirically called 'the abomination of desolation' in Daniel 12:11—and proscribed all Jewish religious festivals and customs. The die was cast.

Some loyalist Jews responded by seeking safety in the wilderness, away from the centres of population, there to found their own religious communes, dedicated to maintaining their own faith. We have a good deal of information about one such commune on the north west shore of the Dead Sea, the Qumran commune, part of whose library has survived. It contains parts of every book in what is now the Old Testament, with the exception of the book of Esther, commentaries on prophetic books, their own revised hymn book modelled on the Psalms, a rule book governing the life of its members, and a document called the War Scroll of the Sons of Light and the Sons of Darkness. This last document, and some of the commentaries, clearly reveal an attitude which we call 'apocalyptic', which has roots in earlier Old Testament material. Faced with an increasingly perplexing world, and often facing persecution for remaining loyal to their faith, the answer of apocalyptic is to give up the present world, to see in current evils the sign that the end of the world is at hand, and to look forward eagerly to the miraculous break-in of the kingdom of God, when all will be transformed, the wicked destroyed and the faithful rewarded. Daniel is the Old Testament example of an apocalyptic book (see pp 134ff). In its present form it comes out of the fires of affliction stoked by Antiochus IV. The darker the age, the more perplexing the times, the greater the appeal of such apocalyptic answers. That has been true right down to the present age.

This has always, however, been the response of the few. Other activist Jews, led by the Maccabean family, were more interested in a political solution to the problems they faced. They took up arms against the persecutor. A highly successful guerrilla campaign led in three years to the expulsion of foreign troops from Jerusalem and the re-dedication of the temple, an event remembered ever since in the joyful festival of *Hanukkah*. After four hundred years of living under foreign occupation, the coming of independence should have led to a revival in the nation's life and a new sense of national unity. Sadly it didn't. The Maccabean success led only to a brief and on the whole inglorious period of independence, marred by internal political and religious squabbles, which ended in rival groups appealing to Rome. This brings us to New Testament times.

We have been trying to trace the history of Israel against its background in the ancient world. We have glanced at the birth of a nation. We have noted a brief period of national greatness and long years of living under foreign occupation. There is nothing particularly strange in such a story. It would hardly warrant more than a few brief paragraphs in a book of world history were it not for the fact that out of it there has come to us a faith, a faith enshrined in a book which has shaped three of the great living religions in the world today—Judaism, Islam and Christianity. It is now time to take a closer look at this book.

3

Exploring the Book

'But I thought it was salt!' That was the tearful cry of a young girl
who had just liberally sprinkled sugar over a plateful of fish and
chips. If only she had known it was sugar, she would have handled
it differently—put it in her tea perhaps. How we handle things
often depends on what we think they are. Nowhere is this more true
than in our approach to the Bible, not least to that part of it which
we call the Old Testament.

If we think it is a book of rules for the good life, our guide to
respectable conduct, then we are going to be in trouble. How, for
example, should you deal with a disobedient child whom you can't
control? If you follow the advice given in Deuteronomy, then you
should drag him along to the local magistrates who will arrange for
him to be stoned to death, 'and you will thereby rid yourselves of this
wickedness' (Deuteronomy 21:21). That is one way of dealing with
the problem. How you would deal with your own conscience there-
after would be another matter. If we think this book tells of some
blood-thirsty god whom Christians can well do without, then we
are going to be in trouble. What more moving statement of the
unchanging love of God can you find than that spoken in God's
name by the poet who wrote Isaiah 49:14-15:

> But Zion says,
> 'The LORD has forsaken me; my LORD has forgotten me.'
> Can a woman forget the infant at her breast,
>   or a mother the child of her womb?
> But should even these forget, I shall never forget you.

If we think this is a book concerned mainly to foretell events which would take place hundreds or indeed thousands of years after it was written, then we are going to be in trouble. How often the book of Daniel has been misused in this way, only to find events disproving the confident forecasts based upon it. Of course you can argue that people had just got hold of the wrong system to explain the mysterious numbers and figures in Daniel, but what is the right system? May it not be that to use the Old Testament, or parts of it, as the basis for a pious guessing game is wholly to mistake its purpose?

If we think this is a book solely for Christians, a book pointing forward always and clearly to Jesus, then we are going to be in trouble. The Old Testament is not only the book of the Christian Church; it is, under another name, the book of another of the world's living religions, Judaism. It belonged to the Jewish people before any Christian ever read it. It would be hard to prove that Christians have a greater right to it, or understand it better, than Jews.

If we think this is a book .... well what is it?

We must first be clear that the Old Testament is *not* a book; it is a bookcase full of books. The sheer size of the Old Testament is daunting, nearly four times the size of the New Testament. If we take the first book in it, the book of Genesis, print it in reasonably sized modern type and format, and bind it within its own covers, we would have a respectably sized paperback to add to any series of religious books; and this is only one out of 39 books according to the way we divide the Old Testament, one out of 22 according to the traditional Jewish way of dividing them. We are handling a bookcase, filled with books richly varied, written by different people at different times and for different purposes. At least a thousand years separates the earliest from the latest material in this bookcase. In it we shall find:

— history books—*eg* Joshua, Judges, Samuel, Kings;
— poetry—*eg* Song of Songs, Lamentations;
— short stories—*eg* Ruth, Esther;
— a hymn book—the Psalms;
— collections of the sayings of wise men, with their shrewd

30

comments on life, its certainties and its mysteries—*eg* Proverbs, Ecclesiastes;
— a tract produced by an underground resistance movement, in an age of persecution—*eg* Daniel;
— a series of books for which there is no easy parallel in our society—the prophets;
— three major or longer books—Isaiah, Jeremiah and Ezekiel;
— and twelve minor or shorter prophetic books—from Hosea to Malachi.

This is only a sample. The range and variety of these books means that we must ask not only 'How are we to approach the Old Testament?', but 'How are we to approach each book in it?' It is no use trying to read highly imaginative poetry as if it were a sober, factual account of events. It is no use going to a hymn with the kind of questions you may rightly ask of a scientific theory. It is no use treating a novel, even a historical novel, as if it were history. If, for example, we believe that the book of Jonah is a straightforward record of events which once happened to a man called Jonah, then we shall have to ask questions about how this man successfully survived, singing hymns, in the belly of a great fish for three days and nights. We shall have to ask questions about the strange climbing plant, the gourd, which sprang up one day to shelter Jonah, and next day lay withered and worm-eaten. But if we approach Jonah as a story, written by a man who combined religious insight with a marvellous sense of humour (imagine thinking that you could run away from God, even at the bottom of the sea!) then we shall ask different and ultimately more serious questions.

But why have these many books, so richly varied in type, authorship and date, been gathered together and presented to us within the covers of one book? What holds them together? After all, to put it mildly, it would be rather odd to gather together in one volume a Shakespearean play, some poems by Burns, chapters from a modern history book, a short story by Neil Gunn, a selection of hymns and a few sermons.

There is first the *unity of history*. All the books in the Old Testament come out of the life and experience of one small nation, the people of Israel. As we have seen, they enable us to sketch in broad outline the history of that nation from the day when its pilgrim forefather, Abram, packed his bags, left Mesopotamia and travelled probably some time between 2000 and 1500 BC until a crisis in that nation's life in the middle of the second century BC. But the unity of history is not enough. If the Old Testament comes to us as the literature of a people, it is not the whole literature of that people. The Old Testament itself makes this perfectly clear. Of the famous lament of David on the deaths of Saul and Jonathan in 2 Samuel 1:19-27, it is said: 'It was written down and may be found in the book of Jashar' (2 Samuel 1:18).

From other references it is clear that this 'Book of Jashar' must have once circulated in Israel as a kind of 'Oxford Book of Hebrew Verse.' Similarly, the narrator in Kings repeatedly refers us for further information to 'the annals of the kings of Israel' or 'the annals of the kings of Judah', books to which he expected his readers to have access. There must have been many books circulating in Old Testament times which are now irretrievably lost; how many we shall never know.

Some books may have survived simply because of their popularity; others may have disappeared by accident. But there came a time when certain books were deliberately chosen for survival. That such a selection was made we know; the only dispute was over which books should be selected. The evidence of that dispute is there in the two forms in which the Old Testament has come down to us: the 39 books which the Reformed church, following Jewish tradition, regarded as the Old Testament; and these 39 plus the books of the Apocrypha, a larger collection which in its Greek form was the Bible of the early church before ever there was a New Testament, and which is still Scripture for the Roman Catholic church. But on what grounds was selection made? It cannot have been on the grounds that the selected books were great literature. In any anthology of 'The Bible designed to be read as Literature', large sections of the

Old Testament would have to be ignored. There is indeed great literature to be found within the Old Testament, for example the book of Job, but the Old Testament as a whole would not survive as great literature either in its original Hebrew form, or in the Authorised Version, or in any modern translation.

We come then to the *unity of faith*. The Old Testament, as we have it, is the result of a verdict passed upon the literature of Israel, not by literary critics, but by men of faith. The books which now survive were selected, because, broadly speaking, they were believed to contain an authentic witness to God's revelation of himself to and in Israel. Notice not only *to* Israel, as if Israel passively received God's revelation, but also *in* Israel, because the opposite side of the coin to God's revelation of himself, is Israel struggling to understand and to live out her destiny as the people of God. The Old Testament speaks of a people facing the grace and the challenge of God in and through their changing experiences. We hear voices joyfully affirming the presence of God, and others agonising over the silence of God. We find some living in the quiet assurance of faith, and others painfully groping their way through the unanswered 'whys' of life. That is not to say that everybody in ancient Israel was deeply religious. Most people in Israel in every age either failed to see God revealing himself, or badly misunderstood what that revelation meant. The Old Testament comes to us not as the record of the many, but out of the faith of the few who saw more deeply and obeyed more truly than their contemporaries. We cannot prove that these few were right, but a true approach to the Old Testament is only open to those who are prepared to risk sharing their faith, seeing themselves as part of the continuing story of 'the people of God' in the world.

It is from the standpoint of that faith we shall now examine the bookcase which is the Old Testament. Traditionally it has three shelves:

— the top shelf contains *'The Law'*
— the middle shelf, *'The Prophets'*
— the bottom shelf, *'The Writings.'*

We shall now take a broad look at each shelf in turn, and sample in greater depth one or two volumes from each shelf.

I

The top shelf contains five books: Genesis, Exodus, Leviticus, Numbers and Deuteronomy. The shelf mark says simply *'The Law.'* 'The Law' is the top shelf because it is for Jewish tradition the final authority for faith, life and conduct, the supremely important section of the library. Indeed the rest of the library is considered to be but commentary on, or further explanation of, what is in 'The Law.'

In many ways it is unfortunate that this top shelf is known to us as 'The Law', because 'law' is a very inadequate translation of the original Hebrew word TORAH. Speak about law in the Old Testament and we immediately think, ah yes, that must be the Ten Commandments and the God who is a stern law-giver, terrifying in his anger and power. So we sing in a hymn:

When God of old came down from heaven,
In power and wrath He came ....

This in sharp contrast to his second coming in Jesus, a coming in power and love! There have been those throughout the history of the church who have not been slow to contrast the Old Testament and the New Testament in terms of 'law' over against 'gospel', anger as opposed to love. This is profoundly to misunderstand both the Old Testament and the New Testament.

In Hebrew TORAH does not mean law in any narrow legalistic sense. It means guidance, teaching, instruction. The book of Proverbs, for example, counsels a young man to listen to the TORAH of his mother, the guidance, the advice she has to offer, born of experience (Proverbs 1: 8). When TORAH was given as a title to the five books on this top shelf, it indicated that here was the teaching, the guidance given to Israel through the revelation of God's character

34

and purposes. Traditionally the key moments in that revelation were believed to be contained in these five books of Moses. Moses is the central figure in much of the material in these books—apart from Genesis—but Moses did not write these books. The closing chapter of Deuteronomy, for example, describes Moses' death and provides us with a brief obituary notice (Deuteronomy 34:1-12). Moreover a book like Genesis has too many rough edges, too many inconsistencies to think of it as coming from the pen of one man. We ought to picture TORAH as being like a great medieval cathedral, hundreds of years in the building, drawing on the labour and the craftsmanship of many generations. Examine it closely and you will see that there is evidence of different architectural styles, yet the whole blends into an impressive unity. TORAH is the cathedral of the central certainties of Israel's faith. We do not come within touching distance of these certainties if we think in terms of 'law' in any narrow or legalistic sense of that word.

What then is TORAH?

(a) TORAH, 'the Law', is a *story*. From the first chapter of Genesis to the end of Deuteronomy, a story is being told. In its present form that story runs all the way from the creation of the world to the point where the people of Israel stand on the verge of their promised land. It is the story of Abraham and the other pilgrim forefathers of Israel, the story of Moses and the wonder of deliverance from slavery in Egypt, the story of God spelling out the basis of his relationship with his people at Mt Sinai, the story of hard and bitter years of wandering in the wilderness. It is a story tracing in the lives of individuals and of a community moments of elation and humiliation, testing and joy, challenge and hope in the conviction that present in every moment there is God.

(b) TORAH, 'the Law' is a *gospel story*. It is a story of good news. Not only does the world come into being and find its meaning through the gracious purposes and the initiative of God, but this same reaching out of God is there in every chapter of the story. This is not the story of people desperately groping their way to a remote and distant God, but of a God who comes to touch their lives and to make himself known to them. What is learned of this God is indeed 'good news.' Think for a moment of the Ten Commandments. Are they not all about what God demands? Yes ... and no; because there is an all important introduction to these demands:

I am the LORD your God who brought you out of Egypt, out of the land of slavery.

(Exodus 20:2; Deuteronomy 5:6)

Words like these echo across the pages of the Old Testament. Prophets and psalmists pick them up. Here is the bedrock of Israel's faith: not what God demands, but what God first gives, not Israel's grasp of God—often a very fragile thing—but God's grasp of Israel.

We must go further. Torah is the story of a people who thought of themselves as 'the people of God.' That does not mean that they were a very godly people, often they were not. It does point to their belief that they had in a peculiar sense been chosen by God. But why did God concern himself with this people? Why did he speak to Abraham? Why did he bring the descendants of Abraham out of enslavement and mould them into a nation? Such questions must have been asked many times, and it is only too easy to give wrong or misleading answers. But listen to Deuteronomy:

It was not because you were more numerous than any other nation that the LORD cared for you and chose you, for you were the smallest of all nations; it was because the LORD loved you and stood by his oath to your forefathers, that he brought you out with his strong hand and redeemed you from the place of slavery, from the power of Pharaoh king of Egypt.

(Deuteronomy 7:7-8)

If we go on to ask why God 'stood by his oath to your forefathers' then, Deuteronomy can only say, 'because he loved your fathers ... ' (Deuteronomy 4:37). TORAH, 'the Law', stakes everything on the love of God. If we then push the question further and ask why God so loved this people, then there is no explanation given; no more than the New Testament explains why 'God loved the world so much that he give his only Son ... ' (John 3:16). As we know from our own experience, love is not something you explain; it is something you gladly accept. TORAH is the good news of such love, the love of God.

(c) TORAH, 'the Law', is the *story of a people's response to God.* In TORAH there are commandments, there are rules governing the whole of life. They range all the way from the broad religious and moral injunctions of the Ten Commandments to specific regulations touching every corner of life, money-lending and sanitation, sexual relationships and building contracts, personal injury and war, the correct ways of approaching God in worship. Such commandments and regulations, however, are always thought of as Israel's glad and rightful response to the love of God.

> When in time to come your son asks you, 'What is the meaning of the precepts, statutes, and laws which the LORD our God gave you?' say to him, 'We were Pharaoh's slaves in Egypt, and the LORD brought us out of Egypt with his strong hand. He harrowed the Egyptians including Pharaoh and all his court with mighty signs and portents, as we saw for ourselves. But he led us out from there to bring us into the land and give it to us as he had promised to our forefathers.'
>
> (Deuteronomy 6:20-23)

> It is in the light of this that 'we should keep all these commandments before the LORD our God, as he has commanded us to do.'
>
> (Deuteronomy 6:25)

The command to love echoes across Deuteronomy because love is the only adequate response to love:

> Hear, Israel: the LORD is our God, the LORD our one God; and you must love the LORD your God with all your heart and with all your soul and with all your strength.
>
> (Deuteronomy 6:4-5)

Only thus in love, spelled out in practical, down to earth, everyday terms could Israel live as 'the people of God.' That was never going to be easy, and not surprisingly Israel often failed. But Israel was never allowed to forget that this was her destiny.

Didn't TORAH, 'the Law', however, later become for the Jews a narrow, rigid, soul-destroying kind of legalism? No doubt for some it did, just as the Christian faith has been so perverted by some of its followers. Let us listen rather to a Jew of deep faith who speaks to us in the Psalms:

> I shall heed your law continually, for ever and ever;
> I walk in freedom wherever I will,
> because I have studied your precepts.
> I shall speak of your instruction before kings
>   and shall not be ashamed;
> In your commandments I find continuing delight:
>   I love them with all my heart.
> I am devoted to your commandments;
> I love them and meditate on your statutes.
>
> (Psalm 119:44-48)

Freedom ... joy ... love ... devotion ... great religious words which the New Testament associates with Jesus and the Christian experience. That is what the law, TORAH, meant and to many still means. This is no shallow faith. If it had been, it would never have survived across the centuries in the refugee camps of ancient Babylon, in recurring days of humiliation and persecution, in the ghettos and the gas chambers of Europe. This is part of our inheritance—TORAH, 'the Law.'

Let us stay with this top shelf of our library and take a closer look at one of the books on it, the book of Genesis It falls naturally into two parts (A) Genesis 1-11 and (B) Genesis 12-50.

A

The first eleven chapters of the book have been, and are, the subject of much all too bitter controversy among Christians. What should we expect to find in these chapters—science ... history ... or what? Should we be trying to show that the latest scientific theories about the origin of the universe and the human race confirm, or at least do not contradict, Genesis 1? What about Adam and Eve? Were they the first man and woman in human history? Then there is the flood and Noah's ark. Can we expect an explorer some day to pick up authentic pieces of the ark on some remote mountain peak in Armenia? To questions such as these, Christians of equal sincerity have given, and give, very different answers, and it is no use pretending otherwise.

Let me explain my own approach. Whenever I can I attend concerts, particularly concerts given by a symphony orchestra. Sometimes the music is familiar, sometimes it is unfamiliar. Occasionally it may be the first public performance of a new work. No matter what the music, however, I always find it helpful to buy a programme and to read the programme notes before the concert begins. In this way I am given a lead into what I am going to hear. The programme notes tell me what I should expect to hear in the music. Often they explain what was in the mind of the composer when he wrote the music. Such programme notes, if they are to be at all useful, must be written by someone who is already at home with the music. He may have heard it dozens or hundreds of times; or, if it is a new work, he will at least have studied the score. I find it helpful to think of Genesis 1-11 as just such programme notes, *written by people already familiar with much that we find elsewhere in the Old Testament.* They stand at the beginning of the Old Testament not because they were written first, but because they are our programme notes, our lead into many of the main themes in the Old Testament story. Let us pick out a few of these themes.

We begin with the 'Hymn of Creation' (Genesis 1:1-2:4a). Calling it a 'Hymn' draws attention to two important things about it:

(a) It uses the language and imagery of poetry, not that of the scientific laboratory or of any scientific theory. It is no more concerned with geology, physics or astronomy than Burns was when he wrote:

> My love is like a red red rose,
> That's newly sprung in June ....

To approach it or to try to read it as a scientific account of the origin of the world, can only lead to endless confusion and futile argument. As soon as you think you have got it neatly fitted into the latest scientific theory, be sure that the scientists will come up with another theory!

(b) It is written by faith for faith. It does not attempt to reason or to prove. It simply places before us what it believes to be lasting truths about God, ourselves and the world in which we live.

There were many gods and goddesses in the world in which this hymn was written. There were many stories about how the world began out of a struggle between the gods and goddesses of order and of chaos, many of them identified with what we see around us in the world around us, sun, moon and the various planets, the fertilising rain and the destructive drought, war and sexuality. In this hymn, however, there is only one God; and no struggle—but only a powerful word, 'God said ...... and so it was.' There is no identifying this God with nature or with anything in it. He stands 'beyond' —to use the technical theological word, he is 'transcendent.' This hymn celebrates a God who is different from this world, yet the source of its life, a God infinitely greater than this world of sense and time, yet a God whose purpose shapes and gives meaning to all life.

What of ourselves? At the apex of this world, introduced with strange solemnity and in a very personal way, there we stand, human beings made in the image of God:

> ... in the image of God he created them;
> male and female he created them.   (Genesis 1:27)

What does this 'in the image of God' mean? Partly it may be explained by the words which follow in the Hymn. We have been given dominion over the rest of creation. We are called to share something of the lordship which God exercises. But there is more to it than that. This dominion is God-given and places the human race in a position of personal responsibility not only towards the rest of creation but also towards God. As a Jewish teacher long ago put it: 'Man is of God, and what is more he *knows* he is of God.' It is as we live our life in the light of this knowledge that we are fully human in the way God intended us to be. Our true humanity finds expression not only in our technological know-how, but in prayer, in our ability to listen to what God has to say to us and in our need to respond to him.

After the 'Hymn of Creation' there comes a section to which the New English Bible gives the heading, *'The beginnings of history.'* This is a very misleading heading. When we look at the story of the Garden of Eden in chapters 2-3 it should be obvious that this is not history as we know it. This is no ordinary garden. All attempts to place it on the map of the world, on the basis of the information in Genesis 2:10-14, have proved futile. This is a garden in which we find mysterious, magical trees, 'the tree of life' and 'the tree of the knowledge of good and evil.' There are strange creatures in the garden, a talking serpent and, at the end of the story, the cherubim, a divine security guard with 'sword whirling and flashing to guard the way to the tree of life' (Genesis 3:24). The leading characters in the story do not have personal names: Adam simply means 'man' and Eve means 'life.'

Turn over a few pages and look for a moment at the flood story in Genesis 6-8. Whether Noah's nautical zoo would have floated or successfully ridden out the flood storm, we may leave to the naval experts, but what are we to say about the flood itself? Archaeology provides us with evidence from many city states in Mesopotamia of severely destructive, more or less local floods occurring at different times in history, but no evidence of a flood where the waters 'increased more and more until they covered all the high mountains everywhere under heaven. The water increased until the mountains were covered to a depth of fifteen cubits' (Genesis 7:19-20).

But if there is no evidence for such a flood, what has come down to us from ancient Mesopotamia is a fascinating story called 'the Epic of Gilgamesh.' It is the story of the human search for the secret of immortality. The hero Gilgamesh, after many exciting adventures, tracks down the one man who is said to have achieved such a blessed state. Here is how it came about. For their own good reasons the gods decided to destroy the human race. It was done by a flood. Utnapishtim, however, forewarned by a friendly god, built a boat, took his possessions, his family, the workmen who had built the boat and 'the seed of all living things', and rode out a storm which in its violence terrified even the gods. Like Noah he sends out birds to find out whether the waters were abating; like Noah his first thought after setting foot on dry land is to offer a sacrifice to the gods.

After hearing of Utnapishtim's experience, Gilgamesh receives from him a plant called 'man becomes young in old age.' On the way home however, it is stolen from him by a snake. That people used to believe that the snake had the secret of eternal youth is not surprising since when the snake's skin becomes old and wrinkled, it casts it off.

The plant of life ... the fatal snake ... the man who survives a god-sent flood: such ideas were familiar in the world out of which Genesis 1-11 comes. Like a modern writer or preacher, the authors of Genesis draw on many different sources—the Epic of Gilgamesh is only one of them—and use a rich variety of material to communicate their own God-given insights.

The first eleven chapters of Genesis are not telling of distant events at the beginning of history; they are facing us with what has always been true and still is true about ourselves, our relationship with God and with one another. They use stories to help us grasp such truths, just as Jesus did in his parables. Let us try to trace briefly what these chapters are trying to say to us. Adam is not the first man: he is 'Everyman', you and I, if only we have eyes to see it. In the Hymn of Creation we caught a glimpse of the glory of the human race made 'in the image of God.' The Garden of Eden tells the story of the tragedy at the centre of human life. It tells of something which cuts right to the very depths of our nature, something which advancing civilisation, education, superior technology or concern for the environment can never eradicate—the wrong in normal people. It is not that we long for immortality, as in the Epic of Gilgamesh. The drama in the garden centres not on the tree of life, but on 'the tree of the knowledge of good and evil', a phrase which probably means 'the tree of *all* knowledge.' Placed in a garden to serve God's purposes, 'Adam' decides that he knows better than God. He will go it alone. Mr Know-All will be the master of his own fate. 'Self' not God will direct what he does. He will replace God at the centre of life; he will grasp at what was meant to be forever outwith his reach ... and his world collapses. The Garden of Delight (Eden means 'delight') becomes a garden of harsh disenchantment. Innocence is replaced by the guilty conscience. He hopes for life and finds himself on the way to death. True community is broken by the 'passing the buck' mentality. Adam blames Eve, Eve blames the serpent, and the serpent had earlier tried to pin the blame on God. Once self has replaced God at the centre of life, it is not surprising that the next story in Genesis 4 is the story of murder, self riding rough-shod over anyone standing in the way.

Two themes keep echoing across the stories, themes to which the rest of the Old Testament is to bear witness again and again. The first is the reality of *judgement*. There is disobedience in the Garden and this leads to expulsion from all its delights. Cain murders a brother and is banished to a precarious life of wandering (Genesis 4). The corruption of the human race increases to such an extent that the flood is sent to wipe it out (Genesis 6-8). People seek to build a tower to their own glory and to secure their own future. They find instead only frustration and confusion (Genesis 11). These chapters take evil with a deadly seriousness. They insist that in a world under God's rule, whoever plays with fire must expect to get burnt.

But that is not the whole or the only truth. Breaking into the sombre chords of tragedy, there is heard the note of hope, witnessing to the graciousness of God. Cain washes his hands of his brother Abel with the classic retort, 'Am I my brother's keeper' (Genesis 4: 9). But God does not wash his hands of Cain the murderer. He judges, yes, but he also puts on Cain a protecting mark (Genesis 4: 15). Cain is sent off wandering into a dangerous, unknown future, but he cannot wander beyond the reach of God's care. The world is engulfed by the destructive flood, but there is one person who 'won the LORD's favour' (Genesis 6:8) to be the beginning of a new humanity. When the storm clouds gather, the rainbow appears in the sky, a constant reminder that never again will God see in total destruction the answer to the chaos created by his problem children (Genesis 9:12-17). 'Glory to man in the highest' is the creed of the tower builders in Genesis 11. They end up a divided and confused human family, but out of that family there is to come one person, Abram, to be the beginning of the people of God. His name was to be changed to the more familiar Abraham (Genesis 17:5) and this is how we shall refer to him.

That is how I read the programme notes of Genesis 1-11. They are there to help us to listen more intelligently to the story of God and ourselves, as that is to unfold across the Bible. We are invited to see ourselves mirrored in the stories. This is our life. Whether you find this approach helpful or not, I hope you may be stimulated to read Genesis 1-11 for yourself. You can read it in about half an hour. You may find yourself faced with questions and gripped by insights which will stay with you for the rest of your life.

B

Let us now take a closer look at the second part of the book of Genesis. Chapters 12-50 take us into a very different world, into the historical roots of the people of Israel. If we ask when the history of the people of God began, then one answer is, on the day when a man called Abraham packed his bags, left the settled security of life in the urban civilisation of Mesopotamia and travelled westward into an unknown future. But are we really in touch with history in these narratives about the founding fathers of the Hebrew people? After all, Abraham (Genesis 12:1-25:18), Isaac (Genesis 26), Jacob (Genesis 25:19-34; 27-35) and Joseph (Genesis 37 and 39-50), and the stories about them, come down to us from the dim and distant beginnings of a nation's memory.

Scholars give very different answers to this question. Some see in the narratives little more than a reflection of the beliefs and experiences of the people of Israel at a much later date. Without going into the various arguments, let me simply say that I do not think we need to be so sceptical. True, the stories were first put down in writing in their present form centuries after the latest possible date for Abraham. In the light, however, of our increasing knowledge of the world of the ancient Near East between the years 2000 and 1500 BC, there is much in the narratives to suggest that their roots are in the social customs and practices of that period, and not that of later Israel.

This does not mean that we can take these chapters and read them as history in our normal sense of that word. Only in one chapter, Genesis 14, is any attempt made to link the events described with significant happenings in the wider world; and that chapter bristles with difficulties. There is no sure identification of the kings whom Abraham is there said to have encountered. Many of the narratives read like family sagas, in the sense in which we talk about the 'Forsyte Saga' by John Galsworthy. Such sagas often concern themselves with quite trivial personal incidents, family intrigues and quarrels, love, jealousy, marriage and death. They reflect and preserve a way of life and a set of values. As such they are of considerable historical value, even when we can't say with any certainty 'this is exactly how it happened.'

Some of the stories seem to tell of the fortunes of tribal groups rather than individuals. The Jacob-Esau stories are a good example. The Jacob of some of the stories represents 'the sons of Jacob', *eg* the people of Israel; Esau represents 'the sons of Esau', the Edomites. At their birth their mother Rebecca is told:

Two nations are in your womb,
>   two peoples going their own ways from birth.
One will be stronger than the other;
>   the elder will be servant to the younger.

(Genesis 25:23)

Other stories explain the origin of the worship of God at various important sites throughout the land of Canaan, notably Hebron (Genesis 13:18), Shechem (Genesis 12:6f; 33:20) and Bethel (Genesis 28:19-22). Many of these places were sacred sites long before Abraham ever came to Canaan. Some of the stories may be little more than the Hebrew versions of much older stories.

Many ingredients seem to have gone into the making of the narratives of Genesis 12-50 in their present form. The most important ingredient, however, is the religious one. Although Abraham is centre stage, this is the story of God's initiative. Why do people emigrate? There are many reasons, personal and political—family quarrels, the call of adventure, job opportunities, the search for political asylum and new freedom. We could suggest such reasons for Abraham leaving Mesopotamia. Other people were on the move at the same time for a variety of reasons. Genesis, however, describes this man's move in a way which is mysteriously different:

> The LORD said to Abram, 'Leave your own country, your kin, and your father's house, and go to a country I will show you ... Abram ... set out as the LORD had bidden him ....

(Genesis 12:1,4)

No explanation is given as to why this call came to Abraham, none except that it was God's move. Certainly it did not come because Abraham was a good guy, whose goodness made him the kind of person God could use and trust. The patriarchs are not idealised figures. Twice Abraham lies to save his own skin (Genesis 12:10-20 and 20); Isaac follows suit (Genesis 26). Jacob is a slippery customer with nothing to learn in the art of one-upmanship, as the Jacob-

Esau and the Jacob-Laban stories make perfectly clear (Genesis 27-33). Joseph in his youth was an insufferable prig. Yet it was to such people that God's call came, and through such people that God's purposes were forwarded. Old Testament writers have few illusions about Israel's goodness, but no doubts about the reality of God's call and the mystery of God's initiative.

Genesis 15 and 17 contain two accounts, probably from different sources, of a covenant made between God and Abraham. A covenant can mean an agreement, a bargain, a treaty drawn up between two parties. This covenant, however, is different. Both accounts go out of their way to stress that this was not a covenant made by Abraham with God, but solely a covenant God made with Abraham. It was a unilateral act. It was God's gift, not a mutual agreement, a gift to Abraham, according to Genesis 15, as he lay unconscious in a deep trance. Genesis 12-50 assumes throughout that there is a special relationship between God and the pilgrim forefathers of the Hebrew nation, and that the first step in establishing that relationship came from God.

This is *the story of a promise*. According to Genesis 12 Abraham sets off into the unknown sustained only by a promise, a promise which contains a three-fold strand:

— the promise of land, 'a country that I will show you' (Genesis 12:1)
— the promise of a future 'great nation' (Genesis 12:2)
— the promise of a blessing which will not only come upon Abraham, but which will be shared by 'all the peoples on earth' (Genesis 12:3).

This three-stranded promise echoes and re-echoes across the pages of Genesis. We hear it first in the initial call of Abraham. It is to be repeated to him at various crisis points in his life. After a family quarrel, Lot chooses what seems to be the best of the land for himself, but Abraham hears again the promise of land and of descendants 'countless as the dust on the ground' (Genesis 13:14-15). Troubled

47

with doubts, childless and with a barren aged wife, Abraham is challenged and reassured: 'Look up at the sky, and count the stars, if you can. So many will your descendants be' (Genesis 15:5; 18:18; 22:17). And the promise is repeated to Isaac, to Jacob and to Joseph.

Notice there are two sides to this promise. The one looks inwards to Israel and to its future—a homeland, a great nation. The other looks outwards, believing that what happens in and through Israel is for all nations. These two sides of the promise were often to be in tension in the history of Israel. It was only too easy for Israel to forget that what she was, she was for the sake of others. You don't need to go far in the church to find the same kind of forgetfulness.

This is *the story of faith*. Often in the book of Genesis, God's promise seems to be under threat, undermined by human disobedience or called into question by the harsh realities of life. Indeed the book of Genesis ends with Joseph embalmed and lying in a coffin in a foreign land, outside the land promised to his fathers. Always this was a promise which called for obedience and could only be grasped by faith. Abraham set out in obedience. Everything depended on his being willing to go, and to go in faith that the promise would one day come to fulfilment. Later, at a moment when, humanly speaking, the promise seemed as far away as ever, and indeed incapable of being fulfilled, Abraham is said to have 'put his faith in the LORD, who reckoned it to him as righteousness' (Genesis 15:6); or as we might put it more simply, Abraham trusted God and for that reason he was in a right relationship with God.

It is against this background that we must understand the dramatic story of the 'binding of Isaac' in Genesis 22. Take it out of this context and you can read it as a story protesting against the practice of child sacrifice, a practice not unknown in Canaanite religion, or in the darkest days of the Hebrew people: or it could be a story explaining why a certain spot was regarded as particularly sacred and suitable for the worship of God. But there is far more to it than that. Who is this Isaac whom Abraham is challenged to sacrifice? He is none other than the child born unexpectedly in Sarah's old age, the child who is Abraham's sole guarantee that the promise of future descendants will be fulfilled. If Isaac dies there will be no great nation. This is the supreme test of Abraham's faith. Is he willing to obey God, even when such obedience seems to mean the end of the very promises God has made? Israel had to learn to live with such a faith, a faith which often had to come to terms with unanswerable questions. A later prophet describes it in this way:

> The one who walks in dark places with no light,
> let him trust in the name of the LORD
>   and rely on his God.
>
> (Isaiah 50:10)

That is still part of the life of faith today.

II

It is time now to turn to the middle shelf of our Old Testament bookcase. Its shelf mark reads *'The Prophets'*, or in Hebrew *Nebi'im*. There are two collections of books on this shelf:

(a) The books of Joshua, Judges, 1 and 2 Samuel, and 1 and 2 Kings are called *'The Former Prophets.'* Read through these books and you may at first think it strange that they should be given the label 'Prophets.' True, they do contain accounts of the activities of certain important prophetic personalities in the life of Israel, men such as Samuel, Nathan, Elijah and Elisha, and the prophetess Deborah. Furthermore, tradition claimed that the books were written by prophets: Joshua being responsible for Joshua and Judges; Samuel the author of the books which bear his name; and Jeremiah the author of 1 and 2 Kings. When you read them, however, it is hard to avoid the conclusion that they would be better listed among 'The Historical Books', as in the subject index of the Revised Standard Version. After all, they tell the story of some six centuries in the life of a nation, from the early struggles to settle in the land of Canaan, through the glory of the United Kingdom and Empire of

David and Solomon, to the subsequent tragic break-up into rival northern and southern states which both fell victim, like many other small states, to the power politics of the ancient world. A brief glance, however, at the way in which 1 Kings describes events which took place in the northern kingdom of Israel in the middle of the ninth century BC, must make us ask, 'What kind of history book is this?'

1 Kings 16:16 describes briefly how the commander-in-chief of the Israeli army, a man called Omri, seized power through a successful military *coup d'état*. Omri's twelve year reign is then dealt with in six verses (1 Kings 16:23-28) which note how he founded a new capital city at Samaria and continued in a tradition of religious apostasy. The next six chapters (1 Kings 16:29-22) are allotted to his son and successor Ahab. From sources outside the Bible we know that Omri was a highly successful king by all the political and economic yardsticks we normally use to measure success. His reputation was known and respected far beyond the boundaries of his own country. His immediate neighbours had first hand experience of the efficiency of his military machine. In comparison, his son and successor was something of a weakling. Yet the book of Kings is far more interested in the judicial murder of a peasant called Naboth to clear the way for an extension of Ahab's palace garden, than it is in the military prowess of Omri. It judges what happened to one of Ahab's most persistent critics, the prophet Elijah, near a cave on a deserted hillside, to be of far more significance than all the cabinet and chief of staff meetings in Omri's new capital.

All historians are necessarily selective in the way in which they handle the material at their disposal, but no modern historian would be satisfied with this kind of selection. Indeed on the basis of what we find in Joshua-2 Kings, it is impossible to write anything like a satisfactory history of ancient Israel. The necessary information is just not there. The authors of Kings are well aware of this. Repeatedly they say, 'if you want further information go and consult other sources, such as the annals of the kings of Israel and Judah.' What Joshua–2 Kings do give us is a commentary on, and an interpretation of what was happening in the life of ancient Israel. We can only understand it if we share a particular faith in its values and if its stark challenge comes to us from the lips of the prophets of Israel. It is not unreasonable, therefore, that these historical books should be classified among 'The Prophets.'

(b) There are the books we normally think of when we talk about 'The Prophets': the three *major* (or longer) prophetic books—Isaiah, Jeremiah and Ezekiel: and the twelve *minor* (or shorter) prophetic books—Hosea, Joel, Amos, Obadiah, Jonah, Micah, Nahum, Habbakuk, Zephaniah, Haggai, Zechariah and Malachi. These books contain the record of the teaching and ministry of a succession of men who, from the middle of the eighth century BC, sought in the name of God to face Israel with the true meaning of her existence as the people of God. They were on the whole highly unpopular. Later ages were to treasure their teaching as Scripture, but their own age more often crucified them, if not by outright opposition, then by sheer indifference to their message.

But what is a prophet? It is unfortunate that in everyday use the word 'prophet' tends to describe someone who peers into the unknown future, who hazards guesses as to what is going to happen ... some day. So we talk about prophesying the date or the result of the next General Election. But the signature tune of an Old Testament prophet is not 'I have been consulting my crystal ball', but *'Thus says the LORD.'* He is not concerned with the tall dark stranger who will one day walk through the door into your life, but with God who is present now, as always, facing his people in judgement and in mercy, calling them to repent, giving them hope deep-rooted in the lasting certainties of the unchanging character of their God.

The word which the prophet speaks is always earthed in the particular circumstances of his own day. We can never fully understand it unless we know something about the day and age in which he lived. For different circumstances there is a different word. The prophet Isaiah at the end of the eighth century BC can say:

Like a hovering bird the LORD of Hosts
will be a shield over Jerusalem;

51

he will shield and deliver her,
sparing and rescuing her.

(Isaiah 31:5)

Nearly 120 years later the prophet Jeremiah has this word for a king in Jerusalem, a king desperately hoping for just such protection, for an eleventh hour miracle of deliverance:

Do not delude yourselves by imagining that the Chaldeans will go away and leave you alone. They will not; supposing you were to defeat the whole Chaldean force now fighting against you, and only wounded were left lying in their tents, even they would rise and burn down this city.

(Jeremiah 37:9-10)

Two more sharply contradictory words it would be difficult to find; but both were the authentic word of God spoken to a particular situation through a prophet. Indeed the people in Jerusalem in Jeremiah's day who were merely repeating Isaiah's message of deliverance, were false prophets!

What makes a prophet? The prophets of Israel were people gripped by a sense of divine compulsion. They were not professionals, nor members of the religious establishment. They came from any and every walk of life. They had not chosen to be prophets. They proclaimed the word of God because they had no option. God had laid his hand upon them and they could not shake off his grasp. In some cases we are given a brief glimpse into a moment of encounter with God which becomes the starting point of their ministry:

Amos says simply: ' ... the LORD took me as I followed the flock and it was the LORD who said to me, "Go and prophesy to my people Israel".'

(Amos 7:15)

Isaiah of Jerusalem tells us of that day in the temple when he was overwhelmed by the awesome, disturbing reality of God's presence, and heard a voice saying: 'Whom shall I send? Who will go for us?' I said: 'Here am I! Send me.' He replied: 'Go, tell this people ....'

(Isaiah 6:8-9)

The setting and the detail of such moments of encounter with God vary from prophet to prophet, but out of them comes a man, not rejoicing in some profound religious experience for its own sake, but a man burdened with a message he must proclaim to others. It is as men called to be messengers of God's word that the prophets are best understood.

It was no new God who entered the lives of these prophets. They have no new faith, no new religion, no new moral teaching to give to their people. They were conservatives, radical conservatives, challenging the community to take seriously the faith it already professed. They speak in the name of the God who had brought his people out of slavery in Egypt, the God of the covenant, the God who had chosen Israel to be his people. They were aware that people far more often need to be reminded of the truth they already know than to be taught new truths. It is difficult for any religious community to remain true to the riches of its heritage. It is to the neglected elements in Israel's religious heritage that the prophets make their appeal.

Let me give you one example. The prophets, in the main, faced a very different situation from that which faces most of us today. Their problem was not empty pews, but temples packed with enthusiastic worshippers. If you would understand the faith which led people to crowd into the temple in Jerusalem, read Psalms 46 and 48. They ring with the confidence that Jerusalem is the city of God. There in the temple on Mount Zion, God, the lord of all the world, the ruler of peoples and nations, is present to meet with his worshipping people. In this faith, and with his assurance, the people fling defiance in the face of all their enemies. To quote Luther's paraphrase of Psalm 46: 'A safe stronghold our God is still.'

53

Then one day, the crowds entering the gates into the temple met a man who said to them, 'You keep saying, "This place is the temple of the LORD, the temple of the LORD, the temple of the LORD!" This slogan of yours is a lie; put no trust in it' (Jeremiah 7:4).

It must have seemed to many that Jeremiah with these words was denying the very foundation of their faith. Not so; he was in fact affirming it. It was because Jeremiah passionately believed in the presence of God in the temple at Jerusalem that he was certain the temple was doomed. Yes, God is present, but for a people whose lives are an open affront to the God whom they claim to worship, this can only mean judgement, not comfort. This was what Israel too easily forgot, though it was part of her faith long before Jeremiah spoke.

Every statement we make about God is double-edged. We rejoice in the steadfast love of God, but unless that love is sheer sentimentalism, it is a refining fire. We affirm the presence of God in our lives, but unless that presence is disturbing as well as reassuring, we are blind to its meaning. Israel was often blind and sentimental, though perhaps no more so than we sometimes are. The prophets cut through such sentimentalism and challenged the people to look again at themselves in the light of God; not for their comfort, but so that they might with a new honesty face what it meant to claim to be 'the people of God.'

Let us take a closer look at this as we find it in one of the shorter prophetic books, the book of Amos. Like most prophetic books the book of Amos is not quite what it seems. Read it through carefully and you will find it difficult to think of it as a well-ordered, easily read book, the work of one author. You get the impression that you are hearing a series of brief and often unconnected sermons. This is in fact a book *about* Amos, the surviving record of his witness and his message. Parts of it may have been written by Amos; parts of it come to us through the memory of his followers. Parts of it may reflect the thinking of such followers rather than that of Amos himself. In its final form, as it now lies before us in the Old Testament, it is most likely the work of someone deeply influenced by Amos, someone who lived some time after Amos' day. The book itself divides into three parts:

— chapters 1-6, which contain the message of Amos with its dominant theme of coming judgement;
— chapters 7-9:7, a mixed bag, containing five visions of Amos, the account of one dramatic incident in Amos' life, and further messages of judgement;
— chapter 9:8-15, an epilogue of hope.

When you examine the first part, you will see that it is made up, in the main, of brief sections, often introduced by the key phrase 'Thus says the LORD', or, as the Revised English Bible renders it, 'These are the words of the LORD'; and sometimes ending with a similar though different phrase, 'It is the word of the LORD' (*eg* Amos 1. 3,5,; 2. 1,3). These phrases give us the clue as to what the book of Amos is.

When in ancient Israel you had a message which you wished to send to someone, you couldn't pop a letter into the nearest pillar box, and leave the postal service to do the rest. Instead you had to send a personal messenger, who memorised your message and *delivered it in your words and in your name.*

In Genesis 32:4, Jacob, uncertain of the welcome he will receive from Esau, the brother he had once cheated, sends on ahead messengers who go to Esau and say, 'Thus says your servant Jacob: I have been living with Laban and have stayed there until now. I have acquired oxen, donkeys and sheep, as well as male and female slaves, and I am sending to tell you this, so that I may win your favour.' So when Amos comes to the people and says, 'Thus says the LORD, I … ', he is coming as God's messenger, and speaking in God's name. It is such messages which are the core of the book of Amos.

Of Amos the messenger we know very little. According to the introduction of the book (Amos 1:1), he came from the village of Tekoa in the barren Judean hills, some twelve miles south of Jerusalem. He was a sheep-farmer, probably tending a breed of hardy sheep which produced fine wool. In the one luminous incident from the prophet's life described in the book (Amos 7:10-15), he speaks of himself as 'a herdsman and fig-grower.' He was part-time shepherd, part-time market gardener, certainly not a professional 'religious' man. There were professional 'prophets' in Israel in Amos' day. They had their place in worship in the temples; they acted as religious advisers at court. They were part of the establishment and tended to support and give divine approval to the official party line. You don't bite the hand that feeds you. Amos stoutly denied that he was that kind of prophet. The market price of wool and the weather were no doubt his major concerns until that day when God stepped into his life and said, 'Go and prophesy to my people Israel' (Amos 7:15). It happened sometime towards the middle of the eighth century, but whether his prophetic activity lasted for a day or a week or a year or several years we do not know. If we know little enough about the messenger, the message speaks to us in all its stark and uncompromising challenge.

Imagine yourself part of a predominantly Scottish crowd listening to a soap box orator at the Mound in Edinburgh. An odd fellow from south of the border, to judge by his accent, he begins by calling down judgement upon Germany for war-time atrocities, for the gas chambers of Auschwitz and Belsen; upon Russia for savage, inhuman policies and the deportation of peoples; upon Japan for treating solemn agreements as mere scraps of paper; upon South Africa for the policy of Apartheid and racial discrimination; upon the USA for political corruption and indifference to the world's poor. The crowd are loving it; great stuff, give us more. So he continues, now calling down judgment upon his own people in England for being uncaring and indifferent to the legitimate national aspirations of others. All the Scottish nationalists are now cheering him on. With the crowd eating out of his hand, he suddenly points the finger at his audience: 'the judgement of God', he says, 'is first and foremost upon *you.*'

That is the picture behind the opening section of the book in 1:3-2:8. Amos from Judah in the south harangues a crowd in one of the great market centres in the northern kingdom of Israel. He assumes that this is God's world, all of it, and built into it are certain moral standards which nations flaunt or ignore at their peril. One by one the nations surrounding Israel are called to judgement, mainly for doing the kind of things with which we are sickeningly familiar in the twentieth century. Then he turns the spotlight of God's judgement on his audience. He must have got a shocked and incredulous response.

Judgement on us? Nonsense, we have never had it so good; peace, security, increasing wealth and an expanding economy. But Amos saw the victims of rapid social change and the free market economy:

— *the landless peasants*, evicted on the pretext of trifling debt to make way for the large estates of the new moneyed aristocracy, with their grandiose mansions and holiday homes, 'winter houses and summer residences' (Amos 3:15);
— *the poor*, crushed under foot, with no possibility of redress from a legal system riddled with corruption and bribery (Amos 5:10-12);
— *the cheated customer*, victims of get-rich-quick traders, giving short measure and overcharging (Amos 8:5).

This was a society in which gross self indulgence and callous indifference co-existed side by side with crippling poverty. Amos doesn't pull his punches:

You loll on beds inlaid with ivory and lounge on your couches;
you feast on lambs from the flock and stall-fed calves;
you improvise on the lute and like David invent musical instru
    ments,
you drink wine by the bowlful and anoint yourselves with the
richest of oils;
but at the ruin of Joseph (*ie* the community) you feel no grief.

(Amos 6:4-6)

57

Judgement on us? Nonsense, we are a devout, truly religious people. The temples are packed; pilgrimages to sacred sites are all the rage. But Amos looks at the flourishing religion of his day and dismisses it as a hypocritical charade, an offence against the character of the God whom they claim to be worshipping:

> I spurn with loathing your pilgrim-feasts;
> I take no pleasure in your sacred ceremonies.
> When you bring me your whole-offerings and your grain-offerings
> I shall not accept them,
> nor pay heed to your shared-offerings of stall-fed beasts.
> Spare me the sound of your songs;
> I shall not listen to the strumming of your lutes.
> Instead let justice flow on like a river
> and righteousness like a never-failing torrent.
>
> (Amos 5:21-24)

Without justice and righteousness, without that right ordering of society through which the legitimate needs of all are met, there can be no right worship of God. 'Come to Bethel,' cries Amos, probably mimicking the pilgrim songs of the day, 'Come to Bethel and ... rebel' (Amos 4:4). What a striking comment it is on the values and realism of this man that he can look at a situation which many of us would regard as highly desirable—packed churches, popular religious enthusiasm—and dismiss it in one pungent word, *rebellion* ... rebellion against God.

Judgement on us? Nonsense, we are God's people. He has been good to us in the past, he will be good to us now and in the future. Yes indeed, says Amos, you are God's people—that's the rub:

> You alone I have cared for among all the nations of the world;
> that is why I shall punish you for all your wrong-doing.
>
> (Amos 3:2)

You are God's people, privileged to be so, and therefore the more responsible. Ignore that responsibility and the judgement upon you must be all the greater. Judgement on us? Nonsense, there are even better times coming. There is that great 'day of the LORD' to which we eagerly look forward, a day when God will crush all our enemies and right all wrongs, a day of joy and light. Yes indeed says Amos, there is a coming 'day of the LORD', but it is not the kind of day you are expecting:

> Woe betide those who long for the day of the LORD!
> What will the day of the LORD mean for you?
> It will be darkness, not light;
> it will be as when someone runs from a lion,
> only to be confronted by a bear,
> or as when he enters his house
> and leans with his hand on the wall,
> only to be bitten by a snake.
> The day of the LORD is indeed darkness, not light,
> a day of gloom without a ray of brightness.
>
> (Amos 5:18-20)

Judgement on us? Yes, judgement. Is this then merely Amos parading before us the Old Testament God of anger? Not at all; Amos' message is rooted in an evangelical passion. Amos believes in a God who has showered his goodness upon this people, a God who brought them out of slavery in Egypt, gave them the promised land of Canaan, and continually sent them people of faith to lead and guide them. But his goodness was mistaken for indulgence; his love called no meaningful response. The God of Amos is a God who has repeatedly warned his people, repeatedly called them to repent. Warning after warning is described in chapter 4:6-11, and after each warning ignored there comes the sad, heart-breaking refrain: 'yet you did not come back to me.' This is a people without excuse who have brought God's judgement upon themselves.

In chapters 7-9 there are five visions which come to the prophet. We don't know when they come. Some of them may be closely related to his initial call from God; others may be later. They tell us something both about the messenger and his message.

First, at the heart of each of the visions there stands something anyone might have seen a plague of locusts (Amos 7:1-3), a catastrophic fire sweeping across the landscape (7:4-6), a man with a plumb-line (7:7-9), a basket of summer fruit (8: 1-3), an altar in a temple (9:1). There are no weird, abnormal hallucinations here, only the ordinary things of everyday experience. But the prophet, under God, sees the ordinary become charged with meaning. The basket of ripe summer fruit becomes Israel ripe for judgement—in Hebrew there is a similarity in sound between the word for 'summer fruit' and 'the end.' The plumb-line becomes God's plumb-line set against the life of Israel, showing only too clearly how crooked it is.

Second, the theme of all the visions is coming judgement, but in the case of the first two, the locus plague and the fire, we find Amos fulfilling one of the traditional rôles of the prophet in Israel. He intercedes on behalf of his people. He pleads with God to stay his hand; and we are told 'The LORD relented.' In the other three visions, however, there is no such intercession. Probably they come from a time when Amos, through bitter experience, realised that nothing short of total disaster would break through the complacency of the people. Warnings had been ignored once to often. Judgement was then inexorable, born of God's concern for his people.

Just because this is the judgement of concern, can disaster ever be God's last word? The book of Amos certainly ends on a note of hope (9:8-15), with pictures of national reconstruction. It has often been claimed that this section of the book does not come from Amos, that it undermines the stern realism of his message, and that the language and the ideas are not his. This is certainly possible. But judgement and promise, disaster and hope are closely interwoven in the teaching of many prophets. If Amos did not speak precisely these words to the community at large, he may have shared with his followers his answer to the question, 'And after judgement, what?' If the plumb-line showed only too clearly a crooked wall that had to be demolished, the site could then be cleared for redevelopment.

That then was the word of God coming through the prophet Amos to the people of Israel in the middle of the eighth century BC. Does it still have anything to say to our world, to the church and to us? Surely this at least. If you clearly hear the judgement of God knocking at the door of other people, let Amos remind you that it is insistently knocking ... at *your* door.

We have been looking at one of the shorter prophetic books; let us now turn to one of the longer prophetic books, the book of Jeremiah. Part of the trouble of not really knowing what is in the Bible is that you tend to believe what is commonly said about it and the characters in it. No one has suffered more from this than Jeremiah. Call someone a 'Jeremiah' and you are hardly being complimentary. A 'moaning Minnie' or, in the words of one of Bing Crosby's hit songs, 'a pessimistic character with a crab apple face'—that is the kind of person you mean. It all stems from Jeremiah being traditionally, and wrongly regarded as the author of the book of Lamentations, and of that book being thought of as a sustained whine. It is worth taking a closer look at this man. We know more about him than about any other Old Testament prophet.

He was what we today would call the son of a country manse. He appeared on the Jerusalem scene during the last forty crisis-ridden years of the independent kingdom of Judah, towards the end of the seventh century and the beginning of the sixth century BC. For some time the ruthless Assyrian military machine had dominated the world of the ancient Near East. Might was right—or so it seemed to politicians in Jerusalem. They had politely escorted God to the touchlines of the universe. Whatever he did he was not involved in the deadly game that was being played out. Their attitude is well summarised in the words: 'The LORD will do nothing, neither good nor bad' (Zephaniah 1:12). That is a practical kind of atheism, always far more common than any intellectual denial of the existence of God.

Then came a period of renewed religious nationalism, culminating in a 'solemn League and Covenant', a national reformation headed by the youthful King Josiah, inaugurated in Jerusalem in

621 BC. Henceforth there would be one nation, under one God, worshipped in the one purified national shrine in Jerusalem. The reformation had the widest possible backing, including probably that of Jeremiah. It carried with it great hopes for the future. It failed, not because it was ill-conceived but because of the sheer cussedness of human nature which can take people's noblest religious ideals and turn them into soul-destroying heresies. It was not long before the Assyrian empire collapsed. You can hear something of the sigh of delighted relief which spread across the world in the book of Nahum. Within twenty-five years of the reformation, however, the cream of Jerusalemite society was deported to Babylon, the new power centre of the world: within thirty-five years the national shrine was a charred ruin in a devastated city.

Jeremiah lived through it all. The last we hear of him is in Egypt, where he went, unwillingly, with a group of Jewish refugees. For over forty years, years in which he witnessed the death throes of his people, Jeremiah proclaimed his message 'Thus says the LORD.' These seem to be words of bold and untroubled certainty. What room can there be for doubt or diffidence in 'Thus says the LORD'? Yet room there was. We know very little about the inner life of the Old Testament prophets. Sometimes we hear of their call, sometimes we are given a certain amount of biographical information: but even where the message is clear, the inmost thoughts of the messenger are usually veiled. Jeremiah is the notable exception. Scattered throughout the book in chapters 1-20 there are passages of an intensely personal nature which have been called his 'confessions', his 'Spiritual Diary.' The veil is lifted. Jeremiah stands before us in all the strength and weakness of a vulnerable and sensitive personality. Here we listen not only to the message, but to the stress and strain which the coming of that message brought into this man's life. Here is not only the public preacher, but a man earnestly, agonisingly at prayer. Here we see not only the unflinching courage which challenged and defied the political and religious establishment, but equally the tormenting doubts, the black moods of depression, the bitter honesty which lie behind this outward courage.

This is a man who had enemies. Even without the evidence of his 'Diary', we would know from many an incident in his career that he was a marked man who provoked violent hatred (see *eg* chapters 26 and 28). You can't attack people's most deeply held convictions and remain popular. Again and again we hear him referring to 'the wicked', 'the treacherous', 'the ruthless', 'his persecutors.' Opposition came not only from the religious establishment, but, unexpectedly, from within his own family circle. He is conscious of a whispering campaign:

> Denounce him! Let us denounce him.
> All my friends were on the watch for a false step,
> saying, 'Perhaps he may be tricked;
> then we can catch him and have our revenge on him.'
>
> (Jeremiah 20:10)

There was the tension caused by stark indifference to his message:

> They say to me, 'Where is the word of the LORD?
> Let it come, if it can!'
>
> (Jeremiah 17:15)

This was the opposition not of bigoted fools, but of deeply sincere people who believed, on the best of scriptural grounds, that Jeremiah was a false prophet. The book of Deuteronomy had laid down that, 'When a word spoken by a prophet in the name of the LORD is not fulfilled and does not come true, it is not a word spoken by the LORD. The prophet has spoken presumptuously; have no fear of him.' (Deuteronomy 18:22). Jeremiah was a living illustration of this. He had preached judgement and coming disaster from the beginning of his ministry, and twenty years later nothing had happened. This is a lonely man, lonely because of his commitment to God:

> I have never kept company with revellers,
> never made merry with them;

because I felt your hand upon me I have sat alone,
for you have filled me with indignation.

(Jeremiah 15:17)

The loneliness was increased by a God-decreed celibate life, as unnatural in ancient Israel as polygamy would be in the western world in the twentieth century. It marked him off from other people. A costly part of his prophetic ministry, dramatically indicating that there was no future for the community in which he lived. There was a price to be paid for such loneliness. Starved of much normal human companionship and affection, he is gripped by a bitter spirit of vindictiveness which led him to scream down curses upon his opponents (see *eg* Jeremiah 18:19-23). It is disturbing to listen to this raw hatred. We shall face the same issue when we look at some of the Psalms.

Opposition and loneliness had a profound effect upon Jeremiah. He is driven in upon himself, to examine and re-examine the very foundations of his faith, to scrutinise his own motives and, above all, to pray with an honesty and intensity which is startling. He faces moods of deep personal depression. He bitterly curses the day he came into the world, born to be 'a man doomed to strife with the whole world against me' (Jeremiah 15:10, cf 20:14-18). He wrestles with nagging doubts. Why do the wicked flourish if this is God's world? Why do those who oppose him prosper, while he, God's messenger, is so obviously a failure? Why? ... and he gets a curious answer:

If you have raced with men running on foot
    and they have worn you down,
      how then can you hope to compete with horses?
If in easy country you fall headlong,
      how will you fare in Jordan's dense thickets?

(Jeremiah 12:5)

You think you have a problem, says God to Jeremiah, cheer up, the worst is yet to come. That may be no answer to the question 'Why?', but it is a word which speaks directly to the spiritual travail out of which that 'Why?' came. It assumes that Jeremiah will continue his spiritual pilgrimage even into more difficult situations; but it is only by going on into the darkness that he will find light.

But there was a deeper doubt. Can God really be trusted?

Why then is my pain unending,
and my wound desperate, past all healing?
You are to me like a brook that fails,
    whose waters are not to be relied on.

(Jeremiah 15:18)

These are very poignant words. Jeremiah had earlier spoken confidently to his people of a God who was 'a source of living water' (Jeremiah 2:13), a bubbling spring which would never dry up. Now for him that spring had turned into one of these river beds which carry no water in the heat of the summer when you most need refreshment. The message and the experience of the messenger seemed to be pulling in opposite directions. Bitterly he accuses God of leading him up the garden path, of seducing him and leaving him to become a laughing-stock (Jeremiah 20:7). Jeremiah had faithfully preached the word he had been given, and for all the response he got he might as well have kept his breath to cool his porridge. He reached the point of no return. He decided to quit, only to find that he couldn't.

I am reproached and derided all the time
    for uttering the word of the LORD.
Whenever I said 'I shall not call it to mind
    or speak in his name again,'
then his word became imprisoned within me
    like a fire burning in my heart.
I was weary with holding it under,
    and could endure no more.

(Jeremiah 20:8-9)

It was apparently impossible to go on, but it was more impossible *not* to go on. He is held in God's grip even in the darkness of despair and seeming failure. In the darkness he reaches out, committing his cause to God (Jeremiah 11:20), praying for healing, and at times discovering the flickering light of faith blazing up into new certainty (Jeremiah 20:13).

It is important to notice one thing about these 'Confessions.' In them Jeremiah is not thinking his own thoughts aloud as in some Shakespearean soliloquy. He is praying, praying with an honesty which to some people may seem almost blasphemous. He pours out his whole life to God, the rough as well as the smooth. His curses are prayers, prayers for vengeance. We may shudder, but it was of no small importance that he did pour out his vindictiveness rather than bottling it up inside him, while giving his prayers an air of calm piety. His doubts are shaped into prayers which wrestle with God. In the end such prayers were more spiritually fruitful than the pious platitudes of lesser people. He cries to God from the depths. We who so often carefully tread in the shallows should hesitate before passing judgement on him. He was a man with all the weakness we share, but a man of God.

III

In the introduction to the book of Ecclesiasticus, one of the books of the Apocrypha, Jesus the son of Sirach tells us of his grandfather, 'who had applied himself industriously to the study of the law, the prophets, and the other writings of our ancestors ....' This is the earliest reference we have—Jesus's grandfather must have been in his prime in the early years of the second century BC—to the third shelf in our Old Testament bookcase, a shelf labelled '*The Writings*', Hebrew *Kethubim*. It is possible that the books on this shelf were called 'The Writings', because nobody could think of a better title for them. Certainly this shelf contains a curious mixture of miscellaneous books which won't fit into the other two shelves; very much like the odd sort of books which tend to get pushed into the bottom shelf of any bookcase. Two things in general may be said about the books on this shelf.

(a) 'The Writings', while achieving a certain status as sacred scripture in the Jewish community, never had the central place of authority which Judaism assigned supremely to TORAH and secondarily to 'The Prophets.' This does not mean that these books were not popular reading: far from it. It is a curious fact that the one festival in the Jewish religious year which could not claim the backing of TORAH and the authority of Moses, the festival of *Purim*, whose origin is described in the book of Esther, one of the Writings, became the most popular festival in the calendar. It is still so celebrated in modern Israel; almost like a students' charity procession with floats depicting events in the story and effigies of the 'goodies and the baddies' being paraded through the streets.

(b) For a long time there was considerable doubt as to which books ought to go on this shelf. The Greek version of the Old Testament, which originated in the Greek-speaking Jewish community in Egypt, and became the Bible of the early Christian church, had many more books packed on this shelf, some of the books which are now in the Apocrypha. The limits of 'The Writings' within the Jewish community do not seem to have been fixed until about the end of the first century of the Christian era, when a group of Jewish teachers meeting at the Palestinian resort of Jamnia, decided which books should not have a place on this shelf. Even some of the books which are there, were accepted only after considerable discussion and the voicing of many doubts. This was particularly so in the case of *Esther, Song of Songs* and *Ecclesiastes*.

The first book on the shelf, and the book which sometimes gives its name to the entire collection, is the book of *Psalms*. We are going later to take a closer look at the Psalms (see pp 79ff). For the moment let us simply note that the Psalms are a collection, or rather several collections, of religious poems which became the hymn book of the Jewish people and later of the Christian church. They give voice to the great certainties which Israel lived and relived in worship across the centuries. They embrace the whole range of a people's response to God, from joyous adoration to the agonising cries of perplexity when faith is apparently overwhelmed by the mystery of suffering, the meaninglessness of life and the seeming silence and absence of God.

From Israel at worship we move into the very different world of 'the wise men', in the book of *Proverbs*. Here we find Israel very much part of the wider world of the ancient Near East. There may be little ultimately in common between the religions of Israel, Babylon and Egypt, but in each country there were 'wise men', teachers who spoke much the same language and commented shrewdly on the same subject—human nature in its devious and diverse moods and motives. The purpose of these wise men was to provide sound instruction, down to earth practical advice which would enable people to make a success of their life, both socially and morally. Typical wisdom teaching is a brief two line saying, with the second line either continuing the theme of the first line or looking at the opposite side of the coin. Here are a few examples:

A wise son brings joy to his father;
   a young fool despises his mother.

(Proverbs 15:20)

Whoever refuses correction is his own worst enemy,
   but one who listens to reproof learns sense.

(Proverbs 15:32)

The tongue of a stupid person is his undoing;
   his lips put his life in jeopardy.

(Proverbs 18:7)

Sloth leads to sleep
   and negligence to starvation.

(Proverbs 19:15)

The book of Proverbs is an anthology of such sayings originating in many different circles. Some of the sayings, but by no means all, are attributed to Solomon, at whose court the wise men probably first flourished in Israel.

That the wise men in Israel borrowed freely from a tradition of wisdom which we can document from outside Israel, is undoubted. One brief section in Proverbs, chapters 22:17-24:22 contains thirty sayings, closely paralleled at points by an Egyptian document, the 'Instructions of Amen-em-opet', with its thirty sections. But what Israel borrowed or shared, she made her own. We can see this happening in Proverbs where wisdom becomes part of the religious experience of Israel. The 'fear of the LORD' is claimed to be both the beginning of wisdom and the prize which comes to those who seek wisdom (Proverbs 1:7; 2:2-8). In chapter 8, Lady Wisdom is portrayed as God's darling and delight, created by him before anything else, present with him when he established the ordered universe. There has been a great deal of speculation about the origin of this figure of Wisdom in Proverbs 8, but this much we can say with confidence; if Wisdom is the key to life, then for Israel it cannot be anything other than God's key.

Proverbs 8 is one of several lengthier sections which, instead of giving us brief two line sayings, develop themes. The book ends in chapter 31:10ff with the Golden ABC of the perfect wife—pre woman's lib version—as if to redress the many harsh things which have been said elsewhere in the book about women. For example:

A constant dripping on a rainy day
  that is what a woman's nagging is like
                              (Proverbs 27:15, cf 6:24-27)

One other thing before we leave Proverbs. People need incentives. One of the carrots, which is dangled to entice people to walk in the way of wisdom, need hardly surprise us. Wisdom, so it is claimed, pays dividends, solid, tangible dividends in this life. The modern ad-man could hardly improve on it. Follow wisdom, keep the commandments:

... for long life and years in plenty
    and abundant prosperity will they bring you.

(Proverbs 3:2)

Honour the LORD with your wealth
    and with the first fruits of all your produce;
then your granaries will be filled with grain
    and your vats will brim with new wine.

(Proverbs 3:9-10)

Is it true? Would it be a good thing if it were true? Both *Job* and *Ecclesiastes*, in their very different ways, have doubts about this 'repaid with interest' approach to religion. We shall look at this more closely when we deal with the book of Job.

Moving along the shelf we find four books which are really one book, 1 and 2 Chronicles, Ezra and Nehemiah. They claim to tell the story of Israel from Adam to the destruction of Jerusalem by the Babylonians (1 and 2 Chronicles); then continue the story on into the time when some Jews returned from exile in Babylon to rebuild the city and temple (Ezra, Nehemiah).

We have already seen some other historical books which are rightly classified among the prophets on the second shelf. Not so these books. Although 1 and 2 Chronicles cover the same period as Samuel–Kings, and indeed use these books as one of their sources, the purpose of the Chronicler's history is very different. We must begin by realising the shattering effect which the destruction of Jerusalem by the Babylonians had upon the Jewish people. The last vestige of the once powerful empire of David and Solomon had gone. The temple on Mount Zion, to many a faithful believer an indispensable means of grace, was a charred ruin. Many Jews were scattered in exile far from their homeland.

When the opportunity to return to the homeland came, some of them came back, not to political freedom, but as part of the Persian Empire. Wherein lay the future destiny of this people. The dream of empire had gone. The future lay not in being a nation, but in being a *religious community*. Ezra–Nehemiah tell of the struggle of the returned exiles. First they had to find security and self-respect—and here Nehemiah, who probably came to Jerusalem before Ezra, played the leading rôle. Then they had to define the community's future. In this Ezra is the key figure. At a public assembly in Jerusalem, Ezra read to the community from the TORAH of Moses. Those present solemnly bound themselves, 'to obey God's law given by Moses the servant of God, and to observe and fulfil all the commandments of the LORD our God, his rules and his statutes' (Nehemiah 10:29). But how could such obedience be fostered and guaranteed? There were to be two key elements in this.

(a) It would be nurtured by a faith which would have its roots in the worship of God in a restored temple in Jerusalem. When the Chronicler looks back across the history of his people, he sees it through the eyes of one for whom worship, worship in the Jerusalem temple, is the very centre of life. So he gives us long lists of temple officials, singers and clergy. When he tells the story of David we get not so much a rounded picture of David the man, warts and all, but David the visionary, responsible for securing the site for the temple and planning the details of the building. There is no use complaining about what the Chronicler does not tell us. Here is a man who sees the worship of God as the supreme goal of life, a man who thought of the small religious community gathered in Jerusalem as the true heirs of the empire of David and Solomon. He would have agreed with the Shorter Catechism that man's chief end was to glorify God and to enjoy him for ever.

(b) The threat to such true worship was only too clear—paganism, which gnawing, cancer-like, at the vitals of Israel, had led in the past to the nation's collapse. In the future this new people of God, therefore, must separate themselves from all contamination by this pagan world. Those who had married foreign wives must divorce them. Henceforth inter-marriage with non Jews was to be strictly forbidden (Ezra 10). The protective barriers were going up. This would be a 'saved community', an isolated island of true faith in the midst of a sea of paganism. Thus and only thus could Israel preserve her distinctive identity. A narrow and limited vision? Yes … and no.

Round about the same time as Ezra and Nehemiah were active in Jerusalem, there was a Jewish community in southern Egypt, near modern Assuan on the Nile. They put up no barriers. They tried to integrate themselves fully into their environment. They worshipped their own God, but also paid their respects to the gods and goddesses of their neighbours. They were tolerant, so tolerant that in the end of the day they had nothing distinctive to offer to the world. The future of the Jewish faith did not lie with them. The community we meet in Ezra and Nehemiah believed that it had something distinctive, worth preserving. They sought to preserve it, and they did preserve it, by a policy of religious apartheid. But vital questions remained unanswered. Can you be a 'saved community' without being a 'saving community.' Do God's people exist for themselves or for the world? The Old Testament never fully resolves these tensions: they are with us still. We can solve them all to easily, either by selling out to the world or by handing the world over to the devil.

From these historical books we turn now to five books which have something very different in common. In many Scottish kirks on Communion Sunday, the Old Testament reading will be taken from Isaiah 52:13-53, with its portrait of the 'Suffering Servant';

> … he was pierced for our transgressions,
>   crushed for our iniquities ….

> (Isaiah 53:5)

This passage had originally nothing to do with any such act of worship. It illustrates something which happens not only to particular passages in the Bible, but also to entire books. Whatever their origin, some books become indelibly associated in the minds of the believing community with important occasions in the religious calendar. This happened to five books among the Writings. They are called the five *Megilloth* or festival books.

(1) The book of *Ruth* became prescribed reading for the Festival of Weeks (Deuteronomy 16:9-12) or Pentecost as it was later called.

Originally a joyful harvest festival, it came to be associated also with the giving of the law (TORAH) to Israel at Mount Sinai, the TORAH which marked Israel as being different from other people. The book of Ruth tells a charming and deceptively simple story of faithfulness rewarded. Ruth leaves her own Moabite kinsfolk to go to Bethlehem with her widowed Jewish mother-in-law, Naomi. With a keen eye to the main chance and making good use of accepted social custom, Naomi gets Ruth married to a well to do and highly respectable Jew called Boaz. So all is well that ends well. Ruth bears Boaz a son, Obed, who is the great grandfather of King David. Deceptively simple, because this is not the story of a Jewish girl, but of a widowed Moabite girl; and the Moabites were not exactly flavour of the month in Jewish circles. Ezra demanded the divorce of all non-Jewish, including Moabite, wives. But here is good King David, than whom surely there is no more acceptable Jew, with a non-Jewish, Moabite, great, great granny. Although it is hard to think of the book of Ruth as having been written deliberately to criticise the policy of Ezra, it remains a parable against exclusiveness, a parable singularly appropriate on the day when the Jewish community celebrated its difference from those 'without the law.'

(2) *Songs of Songs* was prescribed reading for Passover, when the community celebrated the miracle of deliverance from slavery in Egypt. It has always been something of a problem book. Its language is not for the prudish. In frank, ancient eastern language it describes human love and sexuality. Its imagery is a far cry from our whispered words of endearment. *He* would hardly be flattered if *she* told him today:

> His arms are golden rods set with topaz,
> his belly a plaque of ivory adorned with sapphires.
> His legs are pillars of marble set on bases of finest gold.
>
> (Song 5:14-15)

She would probably give him a blank look, if *he* said to her

Your hair is like a flock of goats
   streaming down from Mount Gilead;
your teeth are like a flock of ewes
   newly come up from the dipping ....

(Song 6:5-6)

There seems little doubt that the book owes its place in the Old
Testament partly to the fact that tradition, wrongly, made Solomon
its author, and partly to the fact that the book came to be interpreted not literally, but mystically and allegorically in terms of the
relationship between God and Israel, or Christ and the Church, or
God and the human soul. It is hard, however, to believe that this
was its original meaning. True, the marriage relationship is used
elsewhere in the Old Testament, for example in the book of Hosea,
as a model for the bond which unites God and Israel. Nowhere else,
however, do we find in that context the strikingly frank eroticism
which characterises the Song of Songs.

Is it then, perhaps, a collection of eastern wedding songs? Or is
it a drama involving Solomon, a village girl who has been abducted
to the royal harem, and the village boy to whom she remains obdu-
rately faithful? Or is it?......... there have been many suggestions.
It is perhaps best to take it as a collection of poems celebrating
human love and sexuality. To the Old Testament sexuality is God's
gift, to be enjoyed to the full in creative personal relationships. False
asceticism and life-denying prudishness have little place in the thinking of ancient Israel. Just because human love is of God and to be
accepted joyfully in its holiness, so the language of love can be used
by Old Testament writers to describe God's relationship with Israel,
a love nowhere more clearly shown than in the story of the Exodus
from Egypt. It is hardly surprising then that the Song of Songs was
regarded as appropriate reading when the community relived the
Exodus experience every year at the festival of Passover.

(3) *Lamentations* is a collection of five poems which have as their
common theme the destruction of Jerusalem by the Babylonians in
the year 587 BC. Every note on the keyboard of grief is sounded as the

poet—or poets—depict desolation, grief, hunger, the total break-down of society, and the end of much which the Jewish people had regarded as essential to their faith. Yet the book of Lamentations is no sustained whine. It is a book of hope in which we can see faith rising phoenix-like from the very ashes of Jerusalem. Here is tragedy, yes, but not inexplicable tragedy. The poems accept that such tragedy is God-sent, rightly sent because of the faithlessness and rebellion of the community. But God is no sadist. His true nature is steadfast love. He wounds, but he heals. In penitence, therefore, the community looks through and beyond tragedy:

> The LORD's love is surely not exhausted,
>   nor has his compassion failed;
> they are new every morning,
>   so great is his constancy.
> 'The LORD,' I say, 'is all that I have;
> therefore I shall wait for him patiently.'   (Lamentations 3:22-24)

In the Jewish religious calendar, Lamentations found its place on a fast day in the month of Ab, as the nation remembered the events of 587 BC and the later destruction of the city by the Romans in AD 70. Across the centuries, in many bitter moments, the faithful Jew has found that when all else has been destroyed God, remains, even in the midst of tears, and so the future can never be without hope. It is not surprising that in certain Christian liturgies, Lamentations has found its place in the context of the events of Holy Week.

(4) *Ecclesiastes* is a fascinating and puzzling book. In some respects it is typical of the Wisdom teaching which we find in the book of Proverbs. It contains collections of brief sayings, memorable in their shrewdness:

> If a snake bites before it is charmed, the snake charmer loses his
>   fee.   (Ecclesiastes 10:11)

> Do not speak ill of a king when you are at rest,

or of a rich man when you are in your bedroom,
for a bird may carry your voice,
a winged creature may repeat what you say.
(Ecclesiastes 10:20)

He who keeps watching the wind will never sow,
and he who keeps his eye on the clouds will never reap.
(Ecclesiastes 11:4)

In Ecclesiastes, however, such sayings are set within an unusual framework, the product of a restless, questioning mind which has looked at life from all angles and has come to one conclusion: 'Futility, utter futility ... everything is futile' (Ecclesiastes 1:2). The author of the book was probably a professional teacher. Today he might well have been a university professor with a decidedly sceptical turn of mind. When he speaks of everything as being 'futile'— 'vanity' is the more familiar translation—he does not mean that life is not worth living, nor that you can't get a kick out of it. What troubles him is that to ultimate questions about the meaning of life there seem to be no convincing answers. He is not convinced by many of the answers that other people find helpful: they just don't square with his experience. For him, Wisdom, however useful in practical terms, can never unravel the mystery of life. God has become for this man something of a remote, absentee landlord, up there 'in heaven', while he himself struggles along on earth. The challenging and comforting presence of the God of the prophets and of the psalmists has gone. All that remains is for us not to give any unnecessary offence to God, just accept our limitations, ask no unnecessary questions, and get on with the daily business of living. Again and again he comes back to the conclusion:

I know that there is nothing good for anyone except to be happy and live the best life he can while he is alive. Indeed, that everyone should eat and drink and enjoy himself, in return for all his labours, is a gift of God. (Ecclesiastes 3:12-13)

Then comes death, cold and inevitable, and who knows what, if anything, lies beyond its dark horizon?

> Human beings and beasts share one and the same fate: death comes to both alike. They all draw the same breath. Man has no advantage over beast, for everything is futility. All go to the same place: all came from the dust, and to the dust all return. Who knows whether the spirit of a human being goes upward or whether the spirit of a beast goes downward to the earth?
>
> (Ecclesiastes 3:19-21)

The author of Ecclesiastes stands at the end of a long tradition of faith. He probably lived in the third century BC. In him we see the tradition breaking apart, as for many today the Christian tradition is breaking apart. That is why he can speak to the many who find it easier to share his questions than to pretend to certainties they cannot share. By a strange insight, Ecclesiastes is read at the Festival of Tabernacles, the great harvest thanksgiving festival, the dominant note of which in the Old Testament is one of rejoicing in the goodness of God. Perhaps in the midst of joy it sounds what is often a necessary corrective note. At least it is comforting to know that the reflections of a doubting fellow traveller found a place on the bottom shelf of the Old Testament library.

(5) The book of *Esther* claims to tell the story of the events which lie behind the late, but highly popular festival of Purim. It is a book which, because of its gloating spirit of vengeance, raises for many people difficult questions. It is a book, therefore, which we shall come back to when we look at some puzzling books in our Old Testament library (see pp 131ff).

Perhaps the most impressive thing about these five books, each with a place in Israel's worship, is the rich variety of experience they enshrine—openness towards and vindictiveness against the non-Jewish world, the celebration of human and divine love, coping with tragedy, wrestling with the perplexities of faith. In this they point us to one of the continuing values of the Old Testament, a richness of experience which calls into question any narrowness in our vision or in our response to God.

There is one significant omission from this brief survey of the third shelf in our library—the book of *Job*. It demands fuller treatment. We shall come back to it later (see pp 115ff).

The Law, The Prophets and The Writings, a three shelf library, making up what we call the *Old Testament*. That, of course, is a Christian title for this collection of books. The Jewish title is *Tanak*, using the initial letters of the three Hebrew words which describe the different shelves *T*orah, *N*ebi'im and *K*ethubim.

4

A People at Worship

Suppose you found yourself face to face with a visitor from another planet, someone who knew nothing about our planet earth, its past history or its present problems. If he asked you to explain what it means to be a Christian, where would you begin? Would you introduce him first to some of the great credal statements or confessions of faith produced by the church across the centuries? I wouldn't. Would you give him the Bible and tell him to go away and read a Gospel? I wouldn't. Would you put into his hands some popular theological work on the market today? I wouldn't. I would take him to church. Of course he would be puzzled; yet whether it was in the formal dignity of a cathedral service or with a house group sharing worship, there I believe he would be closest to the beating heart of the Christian faith. If we want truly to understand any religion, we must join its followers as they worship. Why do these people worship? What do they do when they gather for worship? What do they say or sing? What thoughts are in the minds of these people as they share in worship? It is no different when we turn to the Old Testament. We come closest to what is most characteristic in the faith of Israel and to what has given it lasting significance when we go to the *Psalms*, our truest guide to Israel at worship.

Just as in any hymn book, many different people and many centuries have made their contribution to the Psalms. Some of the Psalms were first written in response to specific situations of joy or crisis in the life of the community or of some otherwise unknown individual. Some of them may have been written to be part of the liturgy of one of the great annual festivals in Israel's religious year, just as we have hymns written for Christmas or Easter, for Baptism or Communion services. Whatever the origin of the 150 Psalms, however, they all became part of what was to be the hymn book of Israel at worship. They are rich in recurring human experience. In them people in many different situations in life have seen reflected their own hopes and fears, have found words to express their own inner thankfulness or their need for forgiveness, have caught a vision of the unchanging realities which undergird life and have questioned whether that vision can be true for them. All of this was, and is, part of the experience of a community at worship. We are going to look at six Psalms of very varied type. Three of them are Psalms included, in part at least, in the Psalms selected for inclusion in *The Church Hymnary*, third edition: the other three, for one reason or another, were not so included. Sometimes what we deliberately omit from worship tells us as much about what worship means to us, as what we include.

CELEBRATION

Let us begin with a Psalm which in its metrical form—probably the work of a sixteenth century Scottish exile in Geneva—have echoed across the life of the kirk in Scotland. Three different versions of it appear at the beginning of *The Church Hymnary*. Rightly so, for there is no more stirring call to worship than Psalm 100. Brief though it is, the Psalm divides into two sections, A and B.

A

Make a joyful noise to the LORD, all the lands!
    Serve the LORD with gladness!
Come into His presence with singing!
    Know that the LORD is God!

It is He that made us, and we are His;
We are His people, and the sheep of His pasture.

B

Enter His gates with thanksgiving, and His courts with praise!
Give thanks to Him, bless His name!

For the LORD is good;
  His steadfast love endures for ever,
  And His faithfulness to all generations.

Each section, A and B, contains a call to worship, leading into a
statement as to why worship is necessary and appropriate. Each
section is probably, as elsewhere in the Psalms, in the form of a
dialogue between the priest who is leading worship and the congregation. The priest summons the people to worship, 'Make a
joyful noise to the LORD ......', the people respond by confessing
their faith, 'It is He that made us ....' The priest repeats the call
to worship, 'Enter His gates with thanksgiving ...., the people
respond, 'For the LORD is good ......'
Let us look first of all at the call to worship. The keynote of this
call to worship is celebration, joyful, thankful, uninhibited celebration which demands to be shouted out and to be shared. To be shared
by whom? This depends on how we translate the phrase which the
Revised Standard Version renders, 'all the lands.' It can either mean
'all the land', *ie* the whole community of Israel, or it can mean, as
the Revised English Bible translates, 'all the earth.' So the Scottish
metrical version 'All people that on earth do dwell.' Either way,
notice that as the call comes to the worshippers to make their way into
the temple, probably at Jerusalem, they are being reminded that
they are not on their own, nor are they merely members of a gathered
congregation whether it has ten or a hundred or a thousand folk.
They are being called to celebrate as part of a much larger community of faith. They are being invited to do something which reaches
to the very heart of what it means to be truly human. To know this
is to know that worship can never be allowed to be trivial, never
merely congregation centred. To worship is to share with the whole

family of God's people. Nor do we find any tentative, 'Shall we worship God?', but rather a series of challenging commands: 'Make a joyful noise ... Serve ... Come ... Know ... Enter ... Give thanks ... Bless.'

Central to these commands, the one round which all others turn for Israel is the last command in the first section, 'Know that the LORD is God.' The Psalmist's world knew of many gods and goddesses. Each nation or community would have its own patron god. Few people saw anything wrong in paying homage to several gods. After all, various forces shaped a person's life—good fortune and bad luck, fertility and drought, the life-giving rain and disease, war and death. It made sense to acknowledge the various gods and goddesses who were concerned with these different experiences. But worship for the Psalmist meant acknowledging only one God, the LORD, which is our conventional way of rendering in English the personal name by which the Hebrews called God. The nearest we can get to it is *Yahweh*, the Authorised Version 'Jehovah' is quite wrong. Worship reminded the Psalmist, and the congregation, that there was only one centre to life, only one power who shaped, controlled and worked in and through the rich variety of life's experiences. As Psalm 96 puts it:

Great is the LORD and most worthy of praise;
    he is more to be feared than all the gods.
For the gods of the nations are idols every one;
    but the LORD made the heavens.
Majesty and splendour attend him,
    might and beauty are in his sanctuary.   (Psalm 96:4-6)

Worship is the celebration of and the witness to the one who alone makes an ultimate claim on our lives, and in whom alone all meaning, purpose and value are to be found. Amid the many competing claims and pressures in life, worship reminds us that 'the LORD, and the LORD alone, is God.' By sharing in worship we are confessing this faith to the world around us.

We look now at the people's response to this call to worship. There is usually a quite definite reason why we celebrate, as we often do, in life. It may be the family gathered for a family wedding, to welcome a new child into the family circle or to bring in the New Year. It may be the Saturday afternoon triumph of the football team we support, success in examinations or promotion at work. Similarly there were quite definite reasons why worship for Israel was an occasion for joyful celebration, reasons spelled out in the words:

It is He that made us, and we are His;
We are His people, and the sheep of His pasture.

Worship for Israel was not a laborious attempt to climb up to heaven to find some remote, distant God. It was a joyful response to a God who had come, and was always coming to his people. He had made them. He had taken a bunch of dispirited slaves out of Egypt, given them their freedom and moulded them into a nation. They were his people because he had taken the initiative, coming to them in their need, caring for them, leading them and protecting them as a shepherd does his flock. The essence of Israel's faith, the mainspring of her worship, can be summed up in three simple words: 'we are His':

— not because we wanted to be His ... He wanted us;
— not because we deserve to be His ... God alone knows why;
— not because we can be depended upon ... but because He is dependable.

The great realities which Israel never ceased to celebrate, and to marvel at, were the 'steadfast love' and 'faithfulness' of God (cf Psalm 136). The Hebrew word which the Revised Standard Version translated 'steadfast love' (Authorised Version 'mercy', Revised English Version usually 'love'), particularly when linked with the word 'faithfulness', has about it the thought of a dependability which goes far beyond any legal obligation, and of a graciousness which remains constant and unchanging. You can bet on it against all the odds; you can trust it and it will never let you down. This was Israel's experience of God. With whatever needs we come to worship, whatever the hopes or fears we bring with us, worship should lift us from the shifting sands of our ever changing moods, to the bedrock of a faith which has nothing to do with what we are or how we feel. We come to celebrate with a joy which comes from God, rooted in what he is and what he has done for us, a joy which we offer back to him in worship.

> For the LORD is good;
> His steadfast love endures for ever,
> And His faithfulness to all generations.

CREATOR AND CREATURE

Who am I? ... a number on an income tax file or a credit card, husband, father, teacher, colleague, minister, Scot. Notice that these are all ways of describing me in terms of my relationships with others, whether in the family or at work, with an organisation or in the wider community. It is true of all of us that we become the kind of people we are, we discover more about ourselves through out relationship with other people. Many of the problems and the tragedies in life come when, for one reason or another, these relationships are strained or break down. We can ask the same question, however, in a more fundamental sense. Beyond all the particular relationships in which you and I are involved in life, *who am I*? What, if anything, makes me essentially different from the robots that control the assembly lines in a modern 'car factory; or that chimpanzee who can be taught to do some of the things I do? Who are we? The answers which have been given to that question across the centuries are legion and varied. We are ... a mystery ... either an animal or a god ... a tool-making animal ... a political animal ... nature's sole mistake. We are going to look at the answer that came to people as they gathered for worship in ancient Israel. It is an answer which depends from first to last on a relationship. Our guide is Psalm 8:

> LORD our sovereign,
>   how glorious is your name throughout the world!
>
> Your majesty is praised as high as the heavens,
> from the mouths of babes and infants at the breast.
> You have established a bulwark against you
>   to restrain the enemy and the avenger.
>
> When I look up at your heavens, the work of your fingers,
>   at the moon and the stars you have set in place,
> what is a frail mortal, that you should be mindful of him,
>   a human being, that you should take notice of him?
>
> Yet you have made him little less than a god,
>   crowning his head with glory and honour.
> You make him master over all you have made,
>   putting everything in subjection under his feet:
>   all sheep and oxen, all the wild beasts,
>   the birds in the air, the fish in the sea,
> and everything that moves along ocean paths.
>
> LORD our sovereign,
>   how glorious is your name throughout the world.

This Psalm begins and ends, as all true worship must, with God. In echoing words it celebrates the splendour, the Majesty of God. In addressing God as 'our sovereign', he is speaking as a member of the believing community. His first and last words are words of adoration. He is acknowledging a greatness which goes far beyond the limits of his own thoughts. He is humbling himself before a God who calls forth from him a response of wonder and awe. Unless worship is set within the framework of such wonder and awe, there is a very real danger that it can degenerate into a chat-show—I was going to say a harmless chat-show, but it is not harmless—a chat-show in which we tell God all our needs, hopes and fears, and give him fairly explicit instructions as to what we expect him to do about them. It can happen! Just because wonder and awe take us to the heart of worship, it is the child, and the child's natural sense of wonder, which can truly grasp and celebrate the glory of this God who is in control in heaven and on earth, and whose power defies all the forces which threaten his rule and order. This at least is one interpretation of the somewhat obscure second section of the Psalm, some of whose difficulties you will see highlighted by reading the different translations in our English versions.

There are fortunately no such difficulties when we come to the central section of the Psalm which looks at our human life and the strange paradox of our existence when we see ourselves in the light of God. Look up into the night sky, says the Psalmist, sense its ordered immensity, moon and stars; remember that all this is but the effortless work of God, and then in the light of such a God ask, 'who am I?' Who am I?—nothing more than a frail, tiny, insignificant creature. Everything that we have learned since the Psalmist's day about the universe in which we live—its vastness which can be measured, if at all, only in light years, the countless galaxies—has only underlined that we are but tiny specks on a tiny planet. Who are we that the God who made and controls this astonishing universe should give us even a passing thought? Insignificant, frail, yes, but also unique, claims the Psalmist, made 'little less than a god', to share something of God's power, made to be master over all that God has made. We have already seen the same sense of our uniqueness spelled out in different words in the hymn of creation in Genesis 1, with its statement that 'God made human beings in his own image' (Genesis 1:27), made to exercise dominion over the rest of creation. Naturally the Psalmist speaks of such dominion in terms of the limited world of his own experience, sheep and oxen, the birds of the air, the fish in the sea. We would want to extend his list in ways beyond his imagining—instant communications across the globe, space travel, atomic energy, heart transplants ………

I said that we find here a strange paradox in the Psalmist's description of human life. It is the essence of a paradox that it seems to say opposite, contrary things; yet these opposites are needed to balance one another if we are to give the full picture. It is easy to get things out of balance, by coming down on one side or the other.

Tiny, insignificant specks scurrying about on one small planet among the countless planets in the universe, that we certainly are. There are many people today, increasingly conscious of the complexity and vastness of the universe, who find it impossible to believe that the life of this tiny speck can have any ultimate meaning, or that you and I, in ourselves, are of any real or lasting importance. We can't be significant. We are *only* tiny specks. Yet it is we who sense our insignificance, we who probe the mystery of the universe around us, we who use its resources for our own purposes. Rightly we glory in our advancing technology and scientific know-how, with all the possibilities they open up for us. Yet if we are *only* in control, we are living dangerously. We exploit the natural resources of the earth for our own immediate ends and invite ecological disaster. We split the atom and face the possibility of destroying ourselves in a nuclear holocaust. We manage our economy to protect and enhance our own standard of living and contribute to a world dangerously divided between rich and poor.

The strange paradox, claims the Psalmist, is that we are neither merely insignificant, nor merely unique and in control. We are both. This is what we discover in worship as we look at ourselves in the presence of God, and allow our relationship with God to shape our thinking and our living. Far from being an optional extra, worship is the moment of truth for each one of us.

As we bow before the majesty of God, we are humbled, stripped of all human pretensions. To see ourselves in the light of the vision of God is to learn how insignificant we really are, no matter what our standing in the community may be, no matter how self-important we may sometimes pretend to be. If we are not so humbled in worship we are not truly worshipping. Yet it is just at this moment when we face our own insignificance, and are left wondering 'who am I?', that there comes the surprising answer: 'You are important; God does give you more than a passing thought; you share in God's mastery over all that he has made.' We can express that mastery in all kinds of ways, in digging and cultivating a garden, in cooking a meal, in playing a musical instrument, in shaping basic human needs and emotions into the words of a pop song, in helping to transform metal into a car or a wrought iron gate, in drilling for oil or in developing electronics. In many of the things all of us do, we shape and use the world God has entrusted to us. Notice how the Psalm repeatedly emphasises that all of this is none other than God's gift to us. It is God who has made us 'little less than a god', God who crowns us with glory and honour, God who makes us master over all he has made. With all our power and potentiality, we are not independent. We cannot just do as we like. We can try. This Bible is only too grimly aware—as we are or ought to be today—that when we grasp at independence, when we decide to go it alone, accepting no restraints except our own desires and needs, we are on the way to disaster. All that we have and are has been given to us to be used responsibly within the context of the adoration of God the giver. That is why the Psalm ends, as it began not with us, but with God.

LORD our sovereign,
   how glorious is your name throughout the world!

HONESTY AND CONFESSION

The two Psalms we have looked at so far, Psalm 100 and Psalm 8, have this much in common: they are both comparatively brief. Not so our next Psalm, Psalm 106. It has 48 verses in all. It is easy to see why, on the grounds of limitations of space alone, *The Church Hymnary*, third edition, has chosen to print as Hymn 101 only a few selected verses, the first five verses and the last. Here are these verses in the Revised English Bible:

Praise the LORD.

It is good to give thanks to the LORD,
  for his love endures for ever.
Who can tell of the LORD's mighty acts
  and make all his praises heard?

Happy are they who act justly,
  and who do what is right at all times!

Remember me, LORD, when you show favour to your people;
  look on me when you save them,
that I may see the prosperity of your chosen ones,
that I may rejoice in your nation's joy and exult with your own
  people.

Blessed be the LORD, the God of Israel,
  from everlasting to everlasting.
Let all the people say 'Amen.'
  Praise the LORD.

The missing verses, verses 6-47, may seem eminently reasonable
candidates for omission. At first sight they look as if they had no
relevance for us today. They contain a series of historical snapshots,
taken at various points in over 600 years of the history of Israel.
Moreover they are snapshots of some of the more unsavoury incidents
from that history. To omit them, however, is to run the risk of misunderstanding the verses which remain.

The Psalm begins and ends with the cry 'Praise the LORD', or to
echo in English the Hebrew word, 'Hallelujah.' It is a cry of joyful
confidence and praise, grounded in the fact that the Psalmist believes
that what undergirds all life is the 'goodness' and the 'steadfast love'
of God. But notice the question which is asked:

Who can tell of the LORD's mighty acts
  and make all his praises heard?

The answer in the Psalmist's mind may very well be 'no one.' The greatness and the goodness of God are such that none of us can ever adequately describe them or express our thanks for them. It is easy to take them for granted in the midst of the 'busyness' and the routine of daily life. But perhaps there is another reason why we cannot begin truly to praise God. First we need honestly to face up to the truth about ourselves to which the Psalmist is drawing attention in verses 6-47. These verses take a look at Israel's past record and see it as a story of ingratitude, of promises made and forgotten; a story of a people who sang God's praises one day and rebelled against him the next; a story of complaining and jealousy and of divided loyalties. It is a hard-hitting, sordid tale. The Psalmist has no illusions about his people's past. Equally he has no illusions about himself and the generation to which he belongs. For the story he tells is not told to prove that 'the good old days' were really 'the bad old days'; it is told to illustrate what he knows still to be true in his own experience:

Like our fathers we have sinned,
    we have gone astray and done wrong.

This is where realistically he begins his story in verse 6. The present is no different from the past.

Side by side with this grim catalogue of repeated and continuing human failure, however, he sets something else. The people rebelled,

Yet the LORD delivered them for his name's sake,
and so made known his mighty power.

(verse 8)

The people reaped the bitter harvest of their own folly,

Yet when the LORD heard them wail and cry aloud
    he looked with pity on their distress;
he called to mind his covenant with them
    and, in his boundless love, relented.   (verses 44-45)

90

The Psalmist is not interested in giving us merely a catalogue of human failure. As such it could only have been depressing. He sees human failure throwing into splendid relief the unfailing compassion and dependability of God. This is a story of people attempting to slam the door in God's face; and the story of a God who ever keeps the door open. It is only when we see both sides of this story that we understand what confession really means, how it can keep hope alive and lead to the true praise of God.

For many of us confession is one of the most puzzling and unreal things in worship. I don't think we are sure what we are doing or why. We are either invited to share in prayers of confession which are so general and vague that they do not strike home to us personally, or we are left scratching our head and wondering: 'Now, what is it I must confess? ... Well I lost my temper too easily with the kids last Thursday ... or I should have written that letter ...' We try to tot up the credit and deficit columns in our conduct account. Not only is it far from easy to be honest with ourselves as we do this; but even if we could do it, we would only be skirting the fringes of true confession. Confession comes not merely from searching around for certain things that we think we should have done or should not have done, but from *seeing ourselves, our whole life, in the light of our relationship with and our response to God*. To be aware of the generosity of God's steadfast love is to confess the poverty of our own fitful love and our all too frequent lovelessness. To be gripped by the grace of God which deals with us beyond all our deserving is to be driven to confess that that is not how we handle life. This is how Israel in every generation learned the meaning of confession. In worship they listened to a story, and in the light of that story of God's steadfast love, they knew they had failed. According to Luke's Gospel it was when Peter began to sense something of the mystery and wonder of Jesus that he falls on his knees and says, 'Go, Lord, leave me, sinner that I am' (Luke 5:8).

But the link between praise and confession can also be viewed from the opposite end. It is so easy to take all that comes to us for granted: yes, even membership of the church and the faith we profess. We are seldom really thrilled by or truly thankful for the things we take for granted. Genuine thanksgiving springs out of that honest look at ourselves which confession involves. We learn what it means to shout 'Hallelujah', when we realise that all that comes to us in life comes as a gift which we can never deserve; when we know that it is in spite of what we are that we are accepted by God; when we set over against our failing that unfailing love which ever grasps us.

Mary Craig, in her deeply moving book *Blessings,* found, out of her own experience of suffering, an affinity with and a concern for those who survived the horrors of the concentration camps. Noting the remarkable compassion for others which characterised the lives of many of the survivors, she comments: 'Because they had lived with death, they had understood what was essential to life. Their values were the right way up' (*Blessings,* p 110). That is why there are the two contrasting sides in this and in many other Psalms. The light of God's glory reveals the depth of the darkness within us; and that very darkness throws into splendid relief the light of God's glory.

Psalm 106 moves from 'Hallelujah', praise the LORD, to confession, 'we have sinned'; and from confession, 'we have sinned', to 'Hallelujah', praise the LORD. Perhaps our spiritual values are not the right way up unless we similarly journey through the experience to which the whole of the Psalm is pointing us.

BUT WHY, LORD?

It doesn't take long before we realise that there are many situations in life which are difficult, if not impossible, to understand. Things happen to us, or worse still to those we love, things for which there seem to be no possible reason or explanation. We are left haunted by that nagging three letter word ... why? ... why? ... We go to church and sing 'Jesus friend of little children', and return to see on our TV screens the emaciated remains of dying, hunger-crazed children in Ethiopia. We may seek to salve our conscience by contributing to Oxfam or Christian Aid, but that hardly removes the sting from the question as to *why* it is, in a world created by and in the hands of a God of love, that such things happen. It will not answer our unanswered questions, but it may help us to see things in perspective if we realise we are not alone in our perplexity. People of faith have been here before. They have had to face situations of crisis in their own lives or in the life of the community to which they belong, situations which have seemed to call into question everything they believe. They have been left asking with bitterness and bewilderment, why? ... how long, O LORD, will you allow this to continue?

Of the Psalms in the Old Testament, almost one in three are what we call 'laments.' They show us a community or an individual living through just such a crisis. We shall take Psalm 44 as an example of such a community lament. It begins with the people recalling the tradition of faith in which they have been nurtured, the faith handed down from previous generations:

> We have heard for ourselves, God,
> > our forefathers have told us
> > what deeds you did in their time,
> > all your hand accomplished in days of old.

All of Israel's past history pointed clearly to the great things God had done for his people. This heritage of faith had become the glad and proud possession of the present generation. Confidently they gathered in worship to sing:

> My trust is not in my bow,
> > nor will my victory be won by my sword;
> for you deliver us from our foes,
> > you put to confusion those hostile to us.
> In God have we gloried all day long,
> > and we shall praise your name for ever.   (Psalm 44:6-8)

But if this is the story which faith tells, life is now writing another and a very different script:

> Yet you have rejected and humiliated us
>> and no longer lead our armies to battle.
>
> You have given us up to be slaughtered like sheep
>> and scattered us among the nations.
>
> You have exposed us to the contempt of our neighbours,
>> to the gibes and mockery of those about us.
>
>> (Psalm 44:9,11,13)

What has been happening to the community is raising a large question mark against everything that the people had been brought up to believe. The past may be alive with God's mighty acts, with his care for his people, but where is he now and what, if anything, is he doing in the midst of the confusion and the tragedy of the present? Instead of being able to boast of a God who had delivered his people from their enemies, they are reduced to listening to the taunts and the sneers of these enemies.

The situation cries out for an explanation. There was one obvious explanation ready to hand, deep-rooted in Old Testament tradition and central to much of its thinking. The people are being justly punished for their disobedience to God. They have played with fire and are being burnt. But this answer is firmly rejected:

> Though all this has befallen us, we do not forget you
>> and have not been false to your covenant;
> our hearts have not been unfaithful,
>> nor have our feet strayed from your path.
>
>> (Psalm 44:17-18)

It would be quite wrong to dismiss this as arrogant blindness and self deception. The Psalmist is not claiming that the community is perfect. He is claiming that it has been consciously loyal to its religious heritage, and that nothing that it has done, or failed to do, can possibly justify or explain the severity of tragedy that has struck.

In the face of some of life's tragedies we still hear people saying, 'I wonder what he, or she, has done to deserve that?' Often there is not even the beginning of any real understanding until, like the Psalmist, we answer with a firm 'nothing.' Slick and easy answers, however theologically respectable, are of little help if they make no sense of our experience.

The Psalmist instead goes on to argue that it is precisely because they are God's people that they are suffering:

> For your sake we are being done to death all day long,
>> treated like sheep for slaughter.
>>> (Psalm 44:22)

The way of faith for the people has turned out to be the way of suffering. Even to accept it as such, however, leaves unanswered the question ... why must it be so? We find the same in Jesus' experience. He sets his face steadfastly to go to Jerusalem. He knows the way of obedience to God is the costly way of the cross. Yet on the cross, we hear from his lips the words of one of the Old Testament Psalms of lament:

> My God, my God, why have you forsaken me?   (Psalm 22:1)

So this Psalmist is left asking:

> Why do you hide your face,
>> heedless of our misery and our sufferings?   (Psalm 44:24)

To such agonised and perplexing questions there is no answer, only a series of urgent appeals to God to do something:

> Rouse yourself, LORD; why do you sleep?
>> Awake! Do not reject us for ever.
> Arise and come to our aid;
>> for your love's sake deliver us.   (Psalm 44:23,26)

Does the Psalmist really believe that God is asleep? Doesn't another familiar Psalm claim: 'The guardian of Israel never slumbers, never sleeps'? (Psalm 121:4). To the community whose experience we share in Psalm 44, however, it is not obvious that God is awake. They can see no sign of his presence or his activity in their lives. The present is dark and bleak. It seems that either God does not care what happens to them, or he is powerless to do anything about it. Certainly in their hour of crisis the people do not dream of turning to anyone other than God. In the appeal to God to wake up, to prove once again the reality of his steadfast love, we may rightly see faith seeking to hold on to God, in spite of all that seems to point only to a meaningless darkness. We are also, however, listening to a very frank and open expression of the doubts and the uncertainties, the bewilderment and the unanswered questions, which are present in the minds of the people. *And all this is part of worship.*

If I may raise one of my own puzzled 'whys' at this point: why is it that so few Psalms like Psalm 44 have been selected for inclusion in *The Church Hymnary*, third edition, or in most other modern hymn books? Why is it that in the few which are selected, the verses which most strongly express the Psalmist's perplexity, his dark night of the soul, his urgent questions, tend to be omitted. You will see what I mean if you read Psalm 143 from beginning to end, and then notice how its character is completely changed when Hymn 70 uses only verses 1, 6 and 8. All reference to being hunted down by an enemy, all reference to a heart numb with despair has vanished, leaving only a hymn of serene confidence. Do people today, including church members, not share the Psalmist's perplexities? Do *we* not have unanswered questions? Are there not times when life seems meaningless to us and God seems cruelly silent? When we sit in the pew on Sunday and stand up to sing, we seem too often to pretend that such things do not exist. But is God interested only in our certainties, sometimes our pretended certainties, and not in our questions and in our doubts? If you have never felt like saying, 'Rouse yourself, O LORD, why are you asleep?', you are either lucky ... or dishonest. Psalms, such as Psalm 44, can help us to realise that often the best way to keep faith alive, is to let such doubts, questions, confusion and rebellion come out into the open. Should not worship provide one of the places where this can happen. Perhaps we are frightened to share our doubts with one another, believing that they are a sign of weakness, the enemy of faith. They need not be, as we shall see in our next Psalm.

THE PATHWAY TO A DEEPENING FAITH

Assuredly God is good to the upright,
    to those who are pure in heart.

Thus begins Psalm 73, It expresses a conviction which was widely held in Israel, presumably because it made sense of experience for many people. God, they claimed, can be trusted, as those who seek to follow in his ways well know, trusted to give his faithful people all the good things of life. The opposite side of this coin is summed up in the words of Isaiah 48:22, 'There is no *shalom* for the wicked.' The wicked, those who either defy or ignore God, can never prosper either materially or spiritually. All that is meant by the Hebrew word shalom, life in all its rich fulness, can never be theirs. But do things always work out this way? Not, surely, in the world as we know it, nor in the experience of some people in Israel. This is the nub of the problem with which Psalm 73 wrestles, and it does so with rare honesty.

The wicked do enjoy *shalom*, claims this Psalmist. You have only got to look at them. Unscrupulous they may be, but they are healthy, well-fed and carefree. They occupy positions of power in society, and have no hesitation in using that power to feather their own nest and to make life difficult for others. They are immensely popular in the eyes of many who think that this is the way to get on in life. They openly snap their fingers at God. They assume that he neither knows nor cares about what goes on in this world. Not only do they get away with it, but it pays handsome dividends. It would not take much imagination to produce an up-to-date version of this script.

There are many today who believe that it is only suckers who play it by the book, and that if you want to get on in life you must be prepared to cut corners. If others get hurt in the process, too bad, but that is life. There are plenty of examples which seem to prove that they are right.

Looking at it all, the Psalmist is troubled. Indeed he admits to being envious of the wicked. If the only reward for living the godly life is suffering—and the Psalmist seems to have had his share of it—while the consequences of defying God, and making self number one, is prosperity, then it is hard to avoid the conclusion:

> Indeed it was all for nothing I kept my heart pure
>   and washed my hands free from guilt!
>
> (Psalm 73:13)

What is the point of trying to keep the faith? It does not seem to pay any dividends. His faith is very near being shipwrecked; then he hesitates:

> Had I thought to speak in this way,
>   I should have been false to your people.
>
> (Psalm 73:15)

The full implications of what he was tempted to say are beginning to dawn. If there is no point in believing in God, then that means that the whole tradition of faith in which he had been nurtured, is a cruel hoax. All those people, who in every generation had worshipped and sought to serve God in their daily lives, were deluded. We can almost hear him thinking: 'Now, wait a minute, do I really believe that?' His personal doubts are being kept in check by the faith of others. For many of us, this can be very meaningful. It is one of the compelling reasons for being a member of the church. It would be hard to have to go it alone. One of the strong reasons I have for holding to the faith, is the people I have met in and through the fellowship of the church. I would pefer to be proved wrong with some of them, than right with many of those who dismiss the Christian faith as an illusion. At times, the faith and experience of others can be a much needed steadying influence in our own life.

The fact that other people still held fast to their belief in God did not of course by itself solve the Psalmist's problem. He admits that it remained very tough going, hard to think through: 'until I went into God's sanctuary ...' (Psalm 73:17). It was there in the temple, in worship, that something happened   we do not know exactly what—something which brought the Psalmist face to face with the reality of God's presence, and helped him to see himself and his problem in a new light. Out of this experience of worship two things became clear to him:

(1) There came with new clarity the conviction that although the wicked seemed secure and prosperous, their life was built on very fragile foundations. Their success, however real it seemed to them and to other people, was no more than an illusion, as insubstantial as that dream which vanishes as soon as you wake up. Here today, but tomorrow or the next day there comes the awesome and inescapable terror of death. The story of a person's life can never be seen in true perspective, until the final chapter is written.

(2) Worship forced the Psalmist to recognise that his problem was rooted, not simply in the fact that the wicked seemed to prosper in God's world, but in his own inadequate grasp of what faith really meant. His bitter protest against the way life worked out, his envy of the success of the wicked, were saying something about himself. Why had he been envious of the wicked? Didn't this imply that he too believed that faith in God ought to pay some kind of tangible dividends? But why should it? Is it really wise to commend, or to defend faith, in God as a sound investment which will pay off in terms of the good things of this life? Worship opened the Psalmist's eyes to see that the true meaning and justification of faith lay elsewhere. He describes what he discovered in verses 23-26:

Yet I am always with you; you hold my right hand.
You guide me by your counsel and afterwards you will receive

me with glory.
Whom have I in heaven but you?
And having you, I desire nothing else on earth.
Though heart and body fail,
yet God is the rock of my heart, my portion for ever.

There has been a great deal of discussion as to what precisely the Psalmist meant by the words 'and afterwards you will receive me with glory.' Does 'afterwards' mean after this present life, and does 'glory' refer to heaven and some death-transcending spiritual existence in a world beyond? Or is the Psalmist merely claiming that after all the trouble and spiritual agony he has gone through, God will yet honour him in this present life? It is difficult to be certain. Perhaps it hardly matters what we decide at this point. It is far more important to see the drift of this whole section of the Psalm. It makes two all important claims. *First*, that faith does not depend on our grasp of God, but on God's grasp of us: 'You hold my right hand ... You guide me.' If faith depended on our intellect, our feelings, even our commitment, it would indeed be built on shifting sands. It is God who has reached out for us, and will never let go. *Second*, the essence of faith is a relationship with God, in the light of which everything else pales into insignificance. Here the Psalmist reaches the point of seeing that he has no need to be envious. It does not really matter whether those who defy God prosper. Let them prosper. He has something of supreme value which they can never have, his personal relationship with God.

It is, I think, important to see what it was which led the Psalmist to this new and profound insight. If he had not been prepared to wrestle with the hard questions which life threw at him, if he had not been driven to doubt whether faith had any value at all, he would never have broken through to this deeper faith. There is a modern gospel song which says, 'Jesus is the bridge over troubled waters.' This suggests to me that somehow or other, the storms, the troubles, the doubts, the confusions, are things in life which will never really touch you if you are a Christian. I don't believe that. It would be better to speak of Jesus as the presence with us in the midst of troubled waters. Such troubled waters, as the Psalmist discovered, are often our baptism into a deepening faith. On the other hand, notice what the Psalmist does with his troubled questions. Here is a person for whom faith was becoming increasingly fragile. If, obsessed with his doubts, he had cut his links with the people of God and stopped worshipping, the chances are high that his faith would have totally collapsed. A maturing faith may come at the point where we bring to worship the questions with which we are honestly wrestling, there to discover that:

> Though heart and body fail,
>   yet God is the rock of my heart, my portion for ever.

It is no less important that the believing community should be sympathetic to and supportive of those who wrestle with such doubts.

A WORD OF THANKS

It is so basic to our human life. It is one of the things we early try to teach our children, simply to say 'thank you' for what they receive. It can make your day just to hear someone, sometimes quite unexpectedly, say 'thank you.' It is hardly surprising then that we find many Psalms in the Old Testament which are 'thank you' Psalms; psalms in which the worshipper turns to God with a word of thanks for what he believes God has done for him or given to him. We shall take Psalm 30 as an example. One of the marks of a sincere word of thanks is that it usually comes in response to some quite specific thing that happens in our life. The phone rings. A friend is on the line to congratulate you on passing an examination or getting a job, and you immediately respond, 'thank you.' You sit down for a meal. Someone passes you the sugar or the salt or a cup of tea, and you say 'thank you.' So is it with the 'thank you' Psalms. They are not vague or general expressions of thanks, as if someone had come to the Psalmist and said, 'Don't you think that you ought to be thankful for everything in life?' These Psalms usually describe some experience in which the Psalmist, conscious of particular help received, feels driven to say 'thank you.'

The traditional title to Psalm 30 calls it 'a song for the dedication of the temple.' We know of several such acts of dedication or re-dedication of the temple in the history of Israel. It may refer to the re-dedication of the Jerusalem temple after Jewish patriots, in the bitter wars of the second century BC, had achieved partial liberation for their people and had purged the temple of all the hated pagan symbols and associations which had defiled it. This event is still celebrated annually in the Jewish community at the Festival of Hannukah (Dedication). The Psalm itself, however does not give that impression, it reads much more like the account of a very personal experience. The Psalm may have begun life as a personal word of thanks for God's gracious help in the testing circumstances of one man's life, and then later been taken over by the community to express its gratitude on a different occasion. The Psalm speaks of someone living through a time of trouble and distress, and finding in that trouble and distress that his cry for help is answered.

> I shall exalt you, LORD: you have lifted me up
>> and have not let my enemies be jubilant over me.
> LORD, my God, I cried to you and you have healed me.
> You have brought me up, LORD, from Sheol,
> and saved my life as I was sinking into the abyss.
>
> (Psalm 30:1-3)

The language here is fairly general and may be interpreted in different ways.

The Psalmist talks of being 'healed', but healed from what? He describes himself as having been brought up from *Sheol*. Sheol, to the Hebrews, was the cheerless, gloomy underworld, the 'abyss' or the pit, as it is sometimes called. To it there went down after death a ghostly, lifeless wraith, all that was left of the person. It was the kingdom of the dead where all that made life meaningful and worthwhile was at an end. When the Psalmist, however, says that he has been brought up from Sheol, he does not mean that he has been dead and somehow mysteriously come to life again. To the Hebrews any weakening of life, whether it took the form of illness or disease, crippling pain or misery, was regarded as a form of death. This was the enemy of life gathering a person into its clutches. To be on the way down to Sheol is to be suffering from some serious illness, physical or spiritual. What kind of illness afflicts this man we do not know. As in many other Psalms, the Psalmist talks about his 'enemies.' Again we do not know who these enemies are. They may, in this Psalm, be people who, for one reason or another, hate the Psalmist and are taunting him by claiming that his illness is a sure sign that God has deserted him and is punishing him for his sins—a common enough view in the Old Testament. Whatever the nature of his illness, the Psalmist recognises that this is not his only, or his most serious problem.

Before his illness he had been living in a kind of spiritual no-man's land. Carefree and prosperous, he had been supremely self confident. Life was running his way: 'I felt secure and said, "I can never be shaken"' (Psalm 30:6). There is no reason to assume from this that here is a person who has consciously opted for a way of life in which there was little, or no, room for God. He may have been all his life deeply pious, a good, respectable, God-fearing man, regular and sincere in his attendance at worship. But his religion, as he came to recognise, had become a form of self-centredness. It was part of that secure life that he had built for himself; a life which he was convinced nothing could ever threaten. God was there to guarantee it. It is easy to cross the thin dividing line between truly worshipping God for what he is, and using God for our own purposes, to justify our life-style, our own values, our own church.

Then came the crisis. Illness struck. His own carefully protected life collapsed. God seemed to have deserted him: '... you hid your face, I was struck with dismay' (Psalm 30:7). Broken, afraid, stripped of all self-confidence, he cries, out of weakness and need, for God's help. His 'I can never be shaken' is overtaken by 'Hear,

LORD, and be gracious to me; LORD be my helper' (Psalm 30:10).

And in his hour of need, he discovers the miracle of God's grace that brings healing, new life and joy. He comes back from death's door a changed person. So he comes with a word of thanks, not merely to thank God for recovery from illness, but to give thanks for a healing which has gone far beyond his bodily needs. He has been through a kind of conversion experience, which has turned his inner life upside down. He has been set free from seeing self as number one in life, set free to reach out in praise and thanks to God.

There are two aspects of his word of thanks worth noting:

(1) The Psalmist is describing a very personal experience, yet he knows it must be a shared experience, since it can find—and has found across the years—an echo in the lives of other people. He can't remain silent about what has happened to him. Yes, he says, there are times when the going is rough, times when we feel ourselves on the receiving end of God's anger; but just because it is God's anger, it comes not to break but to remake us. When he comes to say 'thank you' to God, he does not do it alone. He calls on others to share with him:

Sing a psalm to the LORD, all you his loyal servants;
give thanks to his holy name.

(Psalm 30:4)

His word of thanks is a way of witnessing to others, of strengthening their faith, of inviting others to join with him in the praise of God. Sadly, for many of us, worship is seldom a real sharing experience. Instead we come, we sit consumer-like in the pew; we take in, we seldom give. We need new patterns and forms of worship which will help us to see worship as a sharing experience, through which we can be strengthened by each other's experience of the grace of God, each responding to the other's invitation to 'sing a psalm to the LORD.'

(2) As a result of this experience and his reflection on it, the Psalmist ends with a *word of thanks which is a promise*. Indebted to God

for renewed life, he knows that this must be no momentary, passing mood. He has been given new life in order that from this point onwards his life may take a new direction:

> You have turned my laments into dancing;
> you have stripped off my sackcloth and clothed me with joy,
> that I may sing psalms to you without ceasing.
> LORD my God, I shall praise you for ever.

(Psalm 30:11-12)

His word of thanks comes out of deep gratitude. Such gratitude can never be exhausted in a few, fleeting words. The praise and thanks which the Psalmist promises to God are as much a question of living as of speaking. In all true worship there will be words of thanks, springing out of our experience of the grace of God and answered prayer. From all true worship there will come a life of joyful, thankful commitment to the service of God.

5

Some Puzzling Books

We have been dipping into the Old Testament as a three shelf
library. In every library there are some favourite books which are
read again and again. There are others which do little more than col-
lect dust. The Old Testament is no different. We all have our favourite
books and passages. We all have those books and passages which we
are happy to leave alone. It may be because they are puzzling, of little seeming relevance to the world as we know it. It may be that
they are just too difficult to understand. It may be that they raise for
us serious moral or spiritual problems. Whatever the reason, we can
all provide our own list of such books. Let us now take a look at
some books which might appear on many such lists, books which,
I suspect, many people have not looked at for some time ... if ever.

There is an edition of the New English Bible which prints parts
of the Old Testament in smaller type, because such parts 'are often of
interest to the specialist rather than to the general reader.' They are
all right for the scholarly professor, but not recommended reading for
the person in the pew! Only one book in the Old Testament has the
dubious honour of being printed entirely in such small type, the
book of *Leviticus*. So let's begin with Leviticus. We don't have far to
look for the difficulties. They are there staring us in the face right
from the beginning. We enter a strange world. The early chapters are
all about different kinds of sacrifices, about rules governing the life
and activities of the priests. It is an alien world to us. There is the
apparently senseless slaughter of bulls, rams and goats, turtle doves
and pigeons; and who today cares, in the same way as Leviticus,
about what happens to the fat and the blood? Then if you have man-
aged to read your way through this encounter with sacrifices, you
find a long list of animals, fish and birds, divided into 'clean' which

you may eat, and 'unclean' which you must not eat. Who in any case would want to eat 'the griffon-vulture, the black vulture, and the bearded vulture; the kite and every kind of crow, the desert owl, the short-eared owl, the long-eared owl, and every kind of hawk ...' (Leviticus 11:13-19). While you would certainly be in trouble today if you tried to eat an osprey, it would not be for the reason Leviticus lays down. If by this time you have had enough and decide to skip to the back page to see how the book ends, you will hardly be reassured, unless you are a dyed in the wool male chauvinist, since the last chapter begins by informing you that, for certain purposes, a man, in financial terms, is worth twice what a woman is worth (Leviticus 27:1-8).

The temptation to hurry on to something more congenial is strong. Let's ask, however, what is the book of Leviticus all about? We are in the world of the priests in ancient Israel who produced and edited the book, gathering together many different traditions from many different sources. These priests are giving their answer to the question, what kind of community must Israel be if she claims to be the people of God? Behind all the strange details, there are certain broad community guidelines worth pondering. Everything Leviticus says springs from the one basic conviction—*here is the people of God*. This isn't a community seeking to discover its identity. It has been given its identity. What is this to mean in terms of everyday living together in community? We are God's people. It follows therefore, says Leviticus, that:

(1) We can't just do what other people do. We are called to be different, an alternative society.

You must not do as they do in Egypt where once you dwelt, nor may you do as they do in Canaan to which I am bringing you; you must not conform to their customs. You must keep my laws and conform faithfully to my statutes.

(Leviticus 18:3-4)

Many things are forbidden in Leviticus because they represent

107

'the ways of the heathen.' What must make the difference, what sets the standard for this community is a simple statement repeated over and over again in the book: 'I am the LORD your God.' It reminds the people of a relationship out of which there must spring a quality of life: 'You shall be holy, for I the LORD your God am holy' (Leviticus 20:7).

Here is an alternative society whose values are to be set by what they know to be true of the God they worship. The word 'holy' means 'set apart', different, because it belongs to God. So what this people knew of the character of God was to be moulded into their daily living: not one or two simple rules which you could keep and then say 'now I have made it', but an awesome vision which was to penetrate into every corner of life. In Leviticus, more than in any other book in the Old Testament, it is difficult to see the wood for the trees, but it is worth looking, because it is asking a question which we must still answer. Where do we take our values from, we who still claim to belong to the people of God? Do we unconsciously accept the values of the society in which we live, the consumer society of mass advertising and the TV screen, the values of success at all costs, or are we disciplined and directed by a vision springing out of our relationship with God?

(2) We acknowledge that everything that we have comes to us as God's gift, and must be used and cherished as such.

The world in which we live is God's, not ours, and has to be handled as God's. This comes through in several different ways in Leviticus. There is the strange custom of the Sabbath year. Every seventh year there was to be no sowing of seed, no pruning of vines, no harvesting. The land was to lie fallow. It was to be a year of 'rest' for the land (see Leviticus 25:1-7). In addition to that, there was to be every fiftieth year, the year of jubilee, with similar rest for the land. During that year, whatever commercial transactions had previously gone on, all landed property was to revert to its original owner or his heirs: 'No land may be sold outright, because the land is mine, and you come to it as aliens and tenants of mine' (Leviticus 25:23). Thus there was to be a constant check on human greed and acquisitiveness. Never were they to be allowed to forget that the land was God's land, there for their use, but not their abuse, there on loan, but never to be used for purely selfish ends.

So was it with life. The Hebrews believed that life was located in the bloodstream, a common enough view, for obvious reasons, among many people. Whatever happened at any sacrifice in ancient Israel, however, the blood was always given to God at the altar. Nor was anyone in the community allowed to eat meat unless the blood had previously been drained from it: 'because the life of a creature is the blood ...' (Leviticus 17:11). People had to learn that there were limits to what they could do. Life was not theirs to dispose of. How we treat our environment, how we handle life, are still urgent issues in our world today.

(3) We must be a caring society. Much is said in Leviticus about respecting the rights of others—by personal honesty (Leviticus 19:11), by business integrity (Leviticus 19:35), by ensuring that there is not one law for the rich and another for the poor (Leviticus 19:15), by refusing to have anything to do with slander or character assassination (Leviticus 19:16). But there is more; there is an active concern to protect the underprivileged and the weak in society.

Those who are disabled, or handicapped in any way, must be treated with consideration: 'Do not treat the deaf with contempt, or put an obstacle in the way of the blind' (Leviticus 19:14). When a fellow countryman is reduced to poverty, you are under obligation to help him. If you advance him money, no interest is to be charged on the loan (Leviticus 25:35). If he is in such dire straits that he is reduced to selling himself into a form of slavery to work off his debts, he is not to be treated harshly as a slave, and his freedom is to be restored to him in the jubilee year (Leviticus 25:39-40). This must be done because all Israelites are in fact God's slaves, to whom he gave freedom by bringing them out of slavery in Egypt (Leviticus 25:42). At harvest time the fields were not to be reaped right to the edge, nor were the vines to be completely stripped, loose ears of corn and fallen grapes were not to be gathered. They were to be left for the poor and the alien (Leviticus 19:9-10).

The ways of other people might be abhorrent, but when an alien settled in the community, 'you must not oppress him. He is to be treated as a native born among you. Love him as yourself, because you were aliens in Egypt. I am the LORD your God' (Leviticus 19:33). Notice the repeated appeal to what God is like to justify such caring conduct. The God they worshipped was the God who had cared for an enslaved people in Egypt, so they must care.

The disabled ... the poor ... the immigrant: how any society treats such people is a fair pointer to the kind of society it is. Leviticus pleads for a caring society. It is in Leviticus that we first hear the words, 'you must love your neighbour as yourself', and also the reason for so doing, 'I am the LORD' (Leviticus 19:18).

(4) Worship must be central to life. The early chapters of Leviticus with their lists of different sacrifices—whole-offerings, grain-offerings, shared-offerings, sin offerings, and guilt offerings—may seem wearisome. We must remember, however, that in the ancient world sacrifice was a natural and indispensable part of worship. These chapters throb with the warm devotion of a worshipping community. Whether you wished to say 'thank you' to God for the good things of life, whether you wished to bring your needs to him, to take a solemn vow in his presence, or to acknowledge your need to be forgiven, you brought the appropriate sacrifice. All of life was set so naturally within the context of such worship, that it was important to know exactly what you were doing when you came with your sacrifice. In and beyond all the detailed regulations, how-ever, the following points are worth noting.

(a) The entire sacrificial system is regarded as God's gift to Israel; part of God's revelation given to the community through Moses. It was never thought of as a means of bribing God or making him change his mind. It was a God-given means of grace. Through it, through what was visibly acted out in worship, assurance of for-giveness, for example, came to the people. When on the great Day of Atonement, described in Leviticus 16, the goat, upon whose head the sins of the community had been confessed, was driven out into the wilderness, forgiveness was not only a fond hope, but a shared reality. True, this system only operated in the case of 'inadvertent sins', ways in which the individual or the community might unconsciously have offended against God, but it was a pointer to that greater assurance, rooted in the nature of God, which you will find expressed in chapter 26. Here Leviticus claims that punishment for rebellion against God is a stern reality which shatters the life of the community. It can neither be averted nor avoided by any shallow repentance. Given true repentance, however, a broken instead of a stubborn spirit, God would remember his gracious dealings with Israel in the past and would keep open a door of hope for the present and for the future.

(b) Worship was always costly to the worshipper. He had to bring the bull or the ram or the goat or the grain for the sacrifice. Not that poverty was any bar to worship. The poor could offer turtle doves or pigeons instead (Leviticus 5:7ff). It was the bringing that counted, not the value of what was brought, the bringing of something which belonged to yourself. So the grace of God and the response of his people met in worship—as they still do.

Called to be different ... acknowledging everything in life as God's gift ... a caring community ... a community for which worship is central ... that is not a bad check-list for those of us who still ask what it means to be the people of God today.

JONAH, A FISHY TALE

The book of *Jonah* is included among the prophetic books in the Old Testament. It is different, however, from other prophetic books. It is not in the main the record of the teaching and preaching of a prophet; it is a story about a prophet ... and what a story it is!

'Go to the great city of Nineveh,' said God to Jonah (Jonah 1:2): so Jonah rushed down to the nearest sea-port and took a one-way ticket on the first ship outward bound in the opposite direction to Spain. Soon the ship was caught in a violent storm. It was all hands on deck and panic, except for Jonah who was sleeping out the storm in his bunk below. The superstitious sailors, after an unsuccessful prayer meeting, decided that someone must have offended against the gods. When it was discovered that that someone was Jonah, on the run from his god, he bravely volunteered to walk the plank. No sooner did he hit the water than the storm ceased. That ought to have been the end of Jonah, but not a bit of it! A large fish gave him temporary accommodation for three days and nights. In his unfamiliar surroundings Jonah kept his spirits up by his own 'Songs of Praise.' Then he found himself spewed out on dry land, back where he began; and the first thing he heard was God saying to him, 'Go to the great city of Nineveh' (Jonah 3:2). This time Jonah went, to preach hell-fire and damnation against what to him was a wicked, pagan city. To his horror the people of Nineveh repented. Worse still, God changed his mind and decided not to destroy them. In high dudgeon, Jonah told God exactly what he thought of him, then stalked off and sat down outside the city. There poor Jonah sweated it out under the blistering sun. So God made a plant grow to give Jonah some shelter. Next day the plant withered. Jonah was not amused. 'What? angry?' said God to Jonah, 'angry about that plant?' 'Yes indeed,' said Jonah. 'So you are sorry about the plant which you didn't even have the trouble of growing,' said God to Jonah, 'should I not be sorry for this great city, its bewildered citizens, not forgetting the livestock.' If Jonah had any answer to that, it has not been recorded. Perhaps it was unprintable!

If you wish to argue that this is a book which we should read as a factual account of something which once happened to a man called Jonah, then good luck to you. It doesn't matter whether you can produce supposed parallels to a man surviving inside a fish; I am not interested in arguing about it; no more than I am interested in attempts to explain away the odd incidents in the book by suggesting, for example, that Jonah really spent three nights at an inn called 'The Sign of the big Fish', or that it was all a dream. There seem to be more important things to be concerned about in the book of Jonah, once you are prepared to read it as a story, a story written, parable-like to bring people face to face with certain challenging home truths.

(1) *It is the story of a prophet on the run from God.* Jonah did not like the word which came to him from God, 'Go to the great city of Nineveh.' Nineveh was not the kind of place to which you would expect a good, respectable,God-fearing Jew to go. Nineveh was evil, the capital of a ruthless totalitarian régime which had been brutal to the Jewish people. There was no doubt what God wanted Jonah to do, but Jonah wasn't having it—so he tried to run away from God.

Perhaps many of us would claim that our problem is just the opposite. So often we don't know what God wants us to do; there is so much in the Bible we don't understand. I wonder if that really is our problem? Yes, there are things in the Bible which I don't understand, things which want to make me raise my eyebrows. It is not, however, the things I don't understand which worry me; it is the things I understand only too well ... and find so difficult to live with. Yes, there are times when I am puzzled as to what God wants me to do, but I suspect that far more often I know only too well what I ought to do, but I am not prepared to do it. 'Go to the great city of Nineveh' ... so Jonah ran in the opposite direction. But as Jonah found out, it is hard to be on the run from God. You are liable to find yourself back where you began, listening to the same challenge. God does not give up very easily.

(2) *It is a story about repentance, the repentance of most unlikely people.* The Old testament prophets had a hard time with their own people. They constantly called upon them to repent, to change their way of life, and just as constantly the people as a whole refused to change. Jeremiah came to the conclusion that they couldn't change, they who prided themselves on being God's people. Now here is Jonah preaching to people whom the Jews despised as incorrigible pagans, the living embodiment of evil. No sooner does he preach than they repent, every Tom, Dick and Harry of them. It wasn't funny: it made you wonder whether God was playing the game according to the rules. The book of Nahum does abide by the rules. In it God is against Ninevah. It is destroyed by the fire of God's judgement while the Jews and other oppressed peoples cheer from the touchlines. That is what ought to have happened in the book of Jonah; but no,

says the writer of this book, that is not how life necessarily works out. Sometimes the people you least expect to repent, repent; just as sometimes the people you would expect to repent, don't. Sometimes you find a true response to God in the most unlikely places, just as sometimes you look for that response in vain among those who claim to be God's people. It wasn't the Pharisees, the most deeply religious folk who responded to Jesus, it was the despised tax-gatherers and sinners. We would be unwise to assume that it is always in the church that we should look for the true response to God's word today. We ought as Christians to be humbled and shamed by the costly compassion and the imaginative concern and commitment daily expressed by many who never darken the door of a church.

(3) *It is a story about God's limitless compassion, and a man's all too limited compassion.* Jonah's response to the repentance of the people of Ninevah is fascinating. He is shocked and deeply angry not only that they had abandoned their evil ways, but that God was prepared to forgive them. He was shocked, but not wholly surprised since in his bones he knew that God was 'gracious and compassionate, long suffering, ever constant, always ready to relent and not to inflict punishment' (Jonah 4:2). It is one thing of course to believe that; it is another to face the consequences of believing it. Did that really mean that all sorts of undesirable heathens and foreigners were about to be welcomed into God's family? 'I'm afraid it does,' said God to Jonah. Can't we draw the line somewhere to ensure that at least God's enemies are beyond the pale of God's compassion? 'No, I'm afraid we can't.' That is the lesson Jonah was being taught through his sorrow and anger over that plant which was here today and gone tomorrow. If he could be sorry over that plant, how much more was God justified in being sorry for Ninevah and its clueless people, not to mention the livestock! Jonah is a story of protest against the barriers that people put up in the name of God. It is easy, of course, to look back at the Old Testament and deplore the narrow and exclusive attitudes found within it, it is much harder to look at ourselves and to recognise the barriers we put up even as we confess a God who breaks down all the barriers: barriers of social snobbery or race

or sex, barriers of our style of respectability. Are we sure we would not be shocked and upset if certain people started flocking into our kirk? We like it the way it is. Is it to expect too much that we should be living signs of God's barrier-breaking compassion, we who would want to claim that we have even greater reason than Jonah for believing that God is indeed 'gracious and compassionate, long-suffering and ever constant'?

It is a marvellous story, told with a sense of humour and touching our experience at many points. Don't waste your time arguing about that fish. That might be just another way of running away from a God whose limitless compassion questions much that we do and are.

JOB, MYSTERY AND MARVEL

It has been called one of the greatest marvels and mysteries in the literature of the world. If we have any sensitivity to language, we can do no other than marvel at the book of *Job*. Read it for yourself in the Revised English Bible. Marvel at the author's mastery of words, his vivid description of mining in chapter 28, of horse, hawk and eagle in chapter 39. Marvel at Job's moving defence of his past life in chapter 31, his sensitive social conscience, his standard of values. You will be hard pushed to find higher standards. Yet as you read, you soon become aware that the text of the book is very difficult. In every modern translation there are more footnotes in this book, drawing your attention to words, phrases and verses whose meaning is uncertain, than in any other book in the Old Testament. The composer Handel may have known what the famous passage in 19:25 meant, beginning 'I know that my redeemer liveth ...', and enshrined that in unforgettable music; but read the same passage in the Jerusalem Bible or the Revised English Bible, and then ask yourself, 'what does it mean?', particularly when all that the Revised English Bible can say about its translation of verse 26 is 'probable reading; Hebrew unintelligible.'

Beyond all the difficulties of detail, however, there lies a deeper question, 'What is the purpose of the book?' Is it simply to explore the problem raised by undeserved suffering, or is it concerned with what kind of God we ought to believe in, or is it ......? Beyond any doubt it is great literature, and like Shakespeare's Hamlet, part of that greatness is that it can mean many different things to different people. It is hard to say this, and this only, is what it must mean. If you want to see what one modern dramatist has made of it, try the play 'J.B.' by Archibald Macleish. There is no substitute, however, for reading the book for yourself and allowing its marvel and its mystery to make their own impression on you.

It is not the easiest of books to come to terms with, so here is a skeleton outline to help you. The book begins (chapters 1-2) with a prose prologue which introduces us to the leading character, Job, the model Hebrew, a man in whom material prosperity and piety walk hand in hand. This is a good man, a man of whom God can be proud. The scene switches to the heavenly council, where the prosecuting counsel (Satan) argues that it is not surprising that Job is good. It pays him to be so. What would happen if the material props to his piety were taken away? God gives permission for this to happen. Tragedy after tragedy befalls Job; yet he remains unshaken, humbly accepting his fate, firm in his trust in God.

From his prologue we move from prose to poetry and to the core of the book in chapters 3-27. These chapters contain three rounds of speeches, in which Job debates the meaning of the tragedy which has befallen him with three friends, Eliphaz, Bildad and Zophar. Job provokes the debate by pouring out all the pent-up bitterness in his soul. Each of the friends react to Job's outburst, and Job vigorously argues with each of them in turn. In the present form of the book there is no third speech from Zophar, but as the New English Bible footnote indicates, part of chapter 27, which sits very uneasily on the lips of Job, may well contain this missing speech. So far it is all very orderly, though it may not be clear where the debate is leading. In chapter 28 we come to a superb poem on wisdom, that wisdom which ultimately lies only within God's ken. If this had appeared in the book of Proverbs it would have occasioned no surprise, but there has been much argument as to what part it plays, if any, in the book of Job.

In chapters 29-31 Job movingly contrasts his once idyllic life with his present misery, and gives a noble defence of his past conduct. Chapter 31 concludes with the words, 'Job's speeches are finished', and there are some who have argued that this was the end of the first draft of the book. Chapters 32-37 introduce a newcomer to the debate, an angry young man called Elihu. A man of many and caustic words, he is equally critical of Job and his friends. He speaks at length, Job all the while remaining uncharacteristically silent. Chapters 38-42:6 contain two speeches from God to Job, speeches worthy of the God who is the source of all poetry. They have seldom, if ever, been surpassed in literature. Each of these speeches is capped by a few hesitant words of submission from Job. The book then ends with a brief prose epilogue which tells how Job, justified by God, has all his former prosperity restored, with interest.

Even this brief outline will show that there are many questions which can be asked about this book. What, for example, is the relationship between the story told in the prologue and the epilogue and the rest of the book. Isn't the character of Job different, accepting and submissive in the opening two chapters, rebellious and bitter in the poems which follow? What about the happy ending; is it a give away? Is it possible that the author of the poems is using for his own purposes an old story, just as Shakespeare often does, as in Hamlet? Then there are the lengthy speeches of Elihu. Do they add anything to the debate? Are they perhaps the second thoughts of the author of the earlier debate between Job and his friends, or have they been added by another writer irritated by the fact that the earlier debate seems to have produced no answers? Suppose, as is reasonable, the climax to the book is to be found in the speeches of God to Job, why are there two speeches and why do they say nothing about the problem which perplexed Job, the apparently meaningless and undeserved suffering of a good man? You might like to try and work out your own answers to such questions. All I want to do is to put flesh and blood on the skeleton outline by drawing attention to two issues which seem to me to be important in the book. I should warn you, however, that every time I read the book, I come away with different thoughts about it. It is that kind of book!

(1) *Job and his friends*. Let's begin with the debate, discussion, argument—call it what you will—between Job and his friends. They *were* his friends; they came to comfort him, they came and, to begin with, sat silently sharing in his suffering. In their different ways they all stand for a viewpoint which has deep roots in the religion of Israel. Eliphaz puts it well in his first speech:

> For consider, has any innocent person ever perished?
> Where have the upright ever been destroyed?   (Job 4:7)

Religion pays dividends. The godly, the innocent prosper in this world; the wicked, the ungodly never prosper. True, says Eliphaz, no one is wholly perfect, therefore trouble is part and parcel of life's experience. If then suffering comes to a godly man, it must be accepted patiently as God's temporary discipline. God wounds, but he will bind up. The good man will know a full, satisfying, and prosperous life. There is a measure of truth in this. It does correspond to some people's experience, or it would never have had such a firm hold on people's thinking in Israel. *But it did not square with Job's experience.* He had good reason to know that the innocent can be torn apart by tragic and meaningless suffering. As for accepting what has happened patiently as part of God's discipline, Job can only protest that God is part of the problem. He feels totally alienated from God. He demands to know why God, for reasons best known to himself, has got his knife into him, why he cruelly and silently mocks his prayers.

As the debate continues, the gulf between Job and his friends widens. They become increasingly hostile, as Job refuses to listen to what to them is reason, supported by religious experience. Rather than admit that their own deep-held convictions may be wrong, they are prepared to rewrite Job's life. Job must have sinned, and sinned grievously. Eliphaz in his last speech goes so far as to accuse

Job of doing the very things which Job had vehemently denied doing in chapter 31. That is not the first, or the last, time that truth has been sacrificed in the name of religion. If the facts won't fit what you believe, so much the worse for the facts! Job, meanwhile, turns increasingly from his uncomprehending friends to a God who seems to be a cruel and capricious enemy, but who must be just and just in a way that goes far beyond what the friends say about him. Urgently Job demands to be allowed to state his case before the Divine Judge. He is certain that from this Judge he would win an absolute discharge. But where can this Divine Judge be found?

> If I go forward, he is not there;
>> if backward, I cannot find him;
>>> When I turn left, I do not descry him
>>> I face right, but I see him not.

(Job 23:8-9, NEB)

Again and again, Job seems to be caught between hope and despair.

The contrast between Job and his friends is instructive.

(a) The friends have too simple a view of the relationship between suffering and evil. You get what you deserve. It is an attitude which dies hard. We hear it in the New Testament: 'Rabbi, why was this man born blind? Who sinned, this man or his parents?' (John 9:2). In reply Jesus says, 'you are asking the wrong question.' But it is still asked. How often people still say, 'I wonder what he, or she, did to deserve that.' The book of Job is an emphatic protest that this is the wrong, often the cruel question to ask. Life is not as simple as that. The innocent do perish. You don't need to look far in our world today to see that that is true. Sometimes it is the most godly folk who carry the heaviest burdens.

(b) The friends have arrived. They speak with untroubled certainty. Nothing must be allowed to question their cherished beliefs. They represent what they believe to be the orthodox viewpoint, and no doubts about it could be entertained. Once you begin to question it, where will it all end? Job, however, is on a pilgrimage, a troubled pilgrimage in search of a deeper faith and a larger vision of God which will make sense of the darkness in which he ponders. It may seem tough then, in the epilogue, when God rounds on Eliphaz and says, 'My anger is aroused against you and your two friends, because, unlike my servant Job, you have not spoken as you ought about me' (Job 42:7). What had the friends done but defend the faith as they had been taught it, defend it against a man who spoke like a faith-destroying heretic? But the book of Job sees the honesty which, in the light of life's experience, is prepared to question and to challenge accepted belief as being more spiritually fruitful than the uncritical repetition of unquestioned beliefs. It assumes, strangely enough, that God is interested in the truth, however disturbing.

(2) *Job and God.* What are we to make of the speeches of God to Job in chapters 38-41? We have seen that one element in Job's agony is that the God he once thought of as a friend, seems to have become a cruel, capricious enemy, heedless of Job's plight, distant and elusive, Job has demanded to state his case before the Divine Judge; he now finds himself facing a Divine Judge who puts him in the dock, firing at him question after question which underline the awesome mystery of God's limitless power and Job's all too human frailty:

Where were you when I laid the earth's foundations?
     Tell me, if you know and understand.
Who fixed its dimensions? Surely you know!
Who stretched a measuring line over it?
On what do its supporting pillars stand?
Who set its corner stone in place,
     while the morning stars sang in chorus
and the sons of God all shouted for joy?

(Job 38:4-7)

Job searches for God; he is found by God. The lines of communication are reopened. The conversation may not take the form that Job expected or wanted, but conversation there is. In a sense nothing is said by God in these speeches which has not already been said in

120

God's name by the friends. But what Job will not accept from those who are out to break him, he does accept in this new relationship with God. Nothing is said about undeserved suffering. There is no attempt to throw Job's 'guilt' in his face. There is no answer to the agonising 'why' with which Job began his protest. But very often the hurt 'whys' of life are not a request for a neat, easily understood answer to life's mysteries, but a plea for help: 'How am I going to cope with this shattering experience?' Job, his questions still unanswered, finds that he can cope in the light of the presence of a God whose all embracing greatness he dimly grasps. You don't need to have all the answers to know the reality of spiritual healing.

HABAKKUK, QUESTIONS AND CERTAINTIES

Martin Luther, who more than most wrestled with the meaning of the Bible, had this to say about the prophets:

> They have a strange way of speaking as if they maintained no particular order but throw all manner of things together, so that it is impossible to grasp their meaning or to accept what they say.

He had a point. It is only because we tend to restrict our diet from the prophets to certain familiar passages used by the New Testament —for example, the 'Immanuel' passage in Isaiah 7:14 and the 'new covenant' passage in Jeremiah 31:31-14—that we fail to appreciate what he is saying. On the whole, the prophetic books in the Old Testament are not most people's favourite reading. I suppose if you asked many members of the kirk what they knew about *Habakkuk*, they would reply 'Habakkuk? Who is Habakkuk?'

The book of Habakkuk is a short book, three chapters in all. It does not take long to read it; but it has its difficulties and its surprises. It is at first sight a curious hotch-potch. There seems little in it of what we might expect from a man introduced as 'the prophet Habakkuk'; no resounding 'the word of the LORD came to me', no 'thus says the LORD.' In chapter 1 we listen in to a conversation which begins with a man giving voice to his perplexities, arguing with God: 'How long, LORD, will you be deaf to my plea?' (Habakkuk 1:2). When we come to chapter 3, we find a prayer, which is really a hymn, extolling the majesty and the graciousness of God. Much of this is similar to material we find elsewhere in the Old Testament, in the Psalms rather than in the prophetic books. This perhaps tells us something about Habakkuk.

We read so much in the prophets which is sharply critical of what went on in worship, that we tend to think of the prophets as radicals, totally opposed to the religious establishment and to all that went on in the Jerusalem temple. That is not the whole story. Sometimes the sharpest criticism can come from within. There were prophets who had a recognised part to play in worship. They spoke God's word to the congregation; they led the people in celebrating the goodness and the greatness of God. Habakkuk was probably one such prophet—they are usually referred to as 'cult prophets.' He shared the faith of his people as that faith was expressed in worship; and he knew such a faith, if honest, had sometimes to live with unanswered questions.

Habakkuk lived towards the end of the seventh century BC. The Assyrian Empire, which had long bullied and exploited the small nations of the ancient Near East, including Judah, had collapsed. You can experience something of the relief and delight with which the news of the collapse of Assyria was welcomed in Jerusalem by reading the book of Nahum. But the Assyrians were soon replaced by the neo-Babylonian imperialism. For Judah it was very much a case of 'out of the frying pan into the fire.' To people of faith, then as now, the urgent question was 'Where is God in all this? How do you believe in God in a world in which naked power and military aggression seem to have the last word?

Habakkuk begins (Habakkuk 1:2-4) by complaining bitterly about the violent, unjust and evil world in which he lives. He may have in mind the corrupt Jerusalemite society of his own day, or he may be thinking of the international scene so long dominated by the ruthless military machine of Assyria. Why, he asks, why doesn't God do something about it … and do it now. 'But I am doing something,' says God, 'the Babylonians (Chaldeans) are on the move, the instruments of my judgement let loose in the world' (Habakkuk 1:5-11). 'That's all right,' says Habakkuk, 'all right as far as it goes, but the Babylonians are just as brutal, rapacious and callous as the empire they have crushed. How are we to square their triumph with what we believe?'

> Your eyes are too pure to look on evil;
>   you cannot countenance wrongdoing.
> Why then do you countenance the treachery of the wicked?
> Why keep silent when they devour those who are more righteous?
>   (Habakkuk 1:13)

To find the devil you know replaced by another devil does not help much.

It is important to note that Habakkuk has problems *just because he believes.* He believes in an all-powerful and righteous God, and the facts of life seem to call this belief into question. So he is forced to agonise with God, to grope for an answer to doubts which spring out of his prayers. It is often the most spiritually sensitive people who are most deeply troubled as they look at the harsh realities of life in the light of what they know of God. Against this background of a prophet trying to live both with his questions and his certainties, the book of Habakkuk has four things to say.

(1) *Hold on.* To some of the doubts and questions that life throws up, there are no slick or easy answers. To pretend otherwise is dishonest. When Habakkuk, compelled by his commitment to truth, persists in looking for an answer, he is told by God, 'Yes, there is an answer. It will be revealed one day; but meanwhile you must wait and wait patiently.' This is what distinguishes people of faith from others. In the famous words of Habakkuk 2:4—words which are to be used with a somewhat different meaning by St Paul (Romans 1:17; Galatians 3:11)—'… the righteous will live by being faithful.'

123

They will hang on in the midst of the storm. They will cling tenaciously to what they know of God. They will be patiently loyal. There may be no neat intellectual answer to the problem they face, but they can live with it, and live triumphantly with it. But it does mean *living with it*: neither on the one hand saying, 'To heck with it, I'm giving up', nor on the other hand, in the smug self-confidence of a shallow faith, turning a blind eye to the searching questions life brings.

(2) *The wrong response*. Habakkuk was convinced that, whatever his perplexities, certain attitudes to life would not do. In chapter 2:6ff we find a series of 'woes.' Basic to them all is the conviction that, in the very nature of things, certain ways of living are inevitably self-destructive. The attitudes attacked are depressingly familiar. Every society has known them and they are with us still:

— greed and unscrupulous ambition ......
— the abuse and corrupting influence of power ......
— the cult of violence ......

It is as if in the midst of the perplexities, Habakkuk had looked at alternative life-styles to that of someone thirled to belief in a God of righteousness, and drawn back saying, 'No, that can't be right.' The things people know they must reject are often as important as the things they accept.

(3) *A vision*. The hymn which we find in chapter 3 may, or may not, have been composed by Habakkuk, but it expresses his faith. At many points of detail the words of the hymn are far from clear, as you may see by comparing any of the modern translations. The central message of the hymn, however, is clear and powerful. It gives expression to a faith nurtured in worship, a faith which Israel gained by experience, 'through all generations' (Habakkuk 3:2). In traditional language it speaks of the God who comes to his people, a God whose power and majesty are written large in creation and in all the varied forces of nature, as well as in the world of people and nations. But this divine power and majesty are allied to compassion. This is

the God who comes to deliver his people, and to crush the wicked (Habakkuk 3:13). Such had been Israel's experience in the past and, unless faith were a delusion, it must still be true. In dark days of perplexity, people like Habakkuk were sustained by a vision:

— a vision of the power and majesty of God to place over against the power and pride of all human claims;

— a vision of the compassion of God to challenge the aggression and cruelty of people. It was a vision which gripped and humbled and kept hope alive.

(4) *The key to triumphant living.* It was this vision which was for Habakkuk the key to life. There are, as we have seen, many passages in the Old Testament which insist that faith pays dividends, good solid material dividends. Obedience to God according to Deuteronomy 28 brings blessing:

A blessing on the fruit of your body, the fruit of your land and cattle, the offspring of your herds and your lambing flocks. A blessing on your basket and your kneading trough.

(Deuteronomy 28:4-5; cf Proverbs 3:9)

But suppose you have to look out on a world in which there seems to be no signs of such a blessing, what then? Listen to Habakkuk:

The fig tree has no buds,
the vines bear no harvest,
the olive crop fails,
the orchard yields no food,
the fold is bereft of its flock,
and there are no cattle in the stalls.
Even so I shall exult in the LORD
and rejoice in the God who saves me.

(Habakkuk 3:17-18)

This is what it means for the righteous to live by being faithful even in the darkest days: not merely a grim hanging on regardless, but exulting, rejoicing, because it is not what God gives which is important, but God himself. The key to life is a relationship with God, a relationship which remains even when all the material props which are thought to support it, have been knocked away. Habakkuk knew that if your vision of God is large enough, it will carry you through life, not grimly but gladly. There is that joyful certainty even in the midst of doubts.

MALACHI, UNCOMFORTABLE QUESTIONS

If you begin reading the Old Testament at Genesis 1, it is highly unlikely that you will ever get as far as *Malachi*. It is the last book in the Old Testament, some 700 pages on from Genesis 1 in most of our Bibles, and it is very brief, 55 verses in all. There is not much that we can say about the author of this book. He didn't even bother to tell us his name. 'Malachi' in Hebrew means 'my messenger', and that could apply to any number of people. The title of the book probably comes from the opening words of the third chapter: 'I am about to send my messenger to clear a path before me.' Certainly this prophet was concerned to clear a path through a wilderness of complacency and misunderstanding. He was determined to face his people with uncomfortable questions about what they believed and how they lived.

The book comes from about the middle of the fifth century BC. Times were hardly inspiring. The exciting days of rebuilding the Jewish community after the return from exile in Babylon were over. The temple had been restored. Jerusalem was again the focus of the nation's religious life. Politically, however, Jerusalem was but one among many provincial centres in the Persian Empire. Life was reasonably stable. The Persians were tolerant. The Jews settled down, keeping alive a tradition of worshipping God, asking and expecting no more. It is tempting to think that if the religious community in Jerusalem had been subjected to a quinquennial visitation, the verdict would have been 'in a reasonably satisfactory state.' But Malachi was not satisfied. He was a teacher concerned so to present the word of the LORD to his people that they would be driven to ask questions, and in the asking be led to take another look at themselves and their sense of values. Let us pick out four issues from his teaching.

(1) *Exploring the love of God.* 'I have shown you love, says the LORD' (Malachi 1:2). Nothing wrong with that surely, sound teaching. Yes, but Malachi's people were not the first, or the last, to ask, 'what precisely does that mean?' 'How have you shown love to us?' Many another prophet would have answered that question by inviting the people to look back across their own history, back to the exodus from Egypt, back to the settlement in the promised land, back to all the evident signs of God's goodness in the past. Not so Malachi. Look out, he says, out into the world of today; look at what has happened disastrously to the Edomites, the descendants of Esau, brother of Jacob, in the Genesis story. 'Jacob I love' is the LORD's reply, 'but Esau I hate' (Malachi 1:2-3).

At this point you may be thinking that your worst suspicions about the Old Testament are being confirmed. Isn't this just another sorry example of that narrow Jewish nationalism which mars its pages? Yes, you will find in many parts of the Old Testament a fierce hatred of the Edomites. One whole prophetic book, the book of Obadiah, strikes this note (cf Psalm 137:7). There was no love lost between these 'brother' nations. No doubt there were faults on both sides, but to the Jew the Edomites became a symbol of all that was ruthless, treacherous and cruel. That, says Malachi, is something which God 'hates' or rejects. To believe that God loves you means, not that you withdraw from the world into some cosy, self-centred religious experience, but that you grasp that this is a world in which for certain attitudes and certain ways of life, there is no future, a world in which 'the LORD's greatness reaches beyond the confines of Israel' (Malachi 1:5). Look out, says Malachi, and you will see signals of God in action, with a love which is as inevitably destructive of evil as it is supportive of good. Now there may be many questions that we would like to ask Malachi at this point, but at least we must follow him in this. If we believe in the love of God, that cannot merely be a statement about our own personal relationship with God, it must be a confession of something which holds good for all of life, for the whole world of peoples and nations ... or it is just meaningless escapism.

(2) *Only the best*. Malachi has some harsh words to say about the religious leaders of the community. He accuses the priests of 'despising God's name', of 'defiling him'; and when the priests ask indignantly 'How have we done this', he replies, 'by offering God shoddy sacrifices, blind, lame, diseased animals which no one in their senses would have the nerve to offer as a present to the local governor' (cf Malachi 1:6ff). It is not that Malachi had a chip on his shoulder about priests. He is disturbed because the priests were failing to live up to their high calling. They had been entrusted with an all important teaching ministry in the community, a ministry which is nowhere more finely described than in Malachi's words:

> For men hang on the words of the priest and seek knowledge and instruction from him, because he is the messenger of the LORD of Hosts.
>
> (Malachi 2:7)

If the community did not receive that knowledge and instruction in the ways of God, then inevitably it would be off course. What teaching was the community receiving at the temple? Just this, that any old thing was good enough for God. In that case, claims Malachi, you would be better to shut up shop, close the temple altogether. Times of course were hard. The priests may well have thought that half a loaf was better than no loaf at all, a lame sheep better than no sheep. At least worship was being maintained. No doubt some people would have been mortally offended if the priests had refused to accept the animal they brought for sacrifice. Behind Malachi's criticism, however, there is the conviction that in worship, as in all else, *only the best is good enough for God*. It is a test worth applying to our congregational life: or are we content to settle for anything so long as it keeps the organisation ticking over happily, avoids unnecessary friction and leaves the finances reasonably respectable?

(3) *Responsible living.* Turning to the community as a whole, Malachi says, 'if you are wondering why your tearful prayers remain unanswered, I can tell you. You have been unfaithful to the wife of your youth, your "partner" to whom you are bound by solemn covenant' (Malachi 2.14). You have done this for the worst of reasons, to marry 'the daughter of a foreign god' (Malachi 2:11), 'in flagrant violation of the regulations which are supposed to govern the life of God's people' (cf Deuteronomy 7:3). It is important to understand Malachi's position here. He is not opposed to mixed marriages on racist grounds. He is opposed for the following reasons:

(a) Such mixed marriages were bound to weaken the religious loyalty of the community. How can children be brought up in the true tradition of Israel's faith in a home which had within it divided religious loyalties?

(b) There is, he claims, cruelty involved in divorcing a wife presumably for no better reason than the seductive charms of a foreign beauty. In a society where the husband had legally absolute right to divorce his wife, but the wife no such corresponding right, it is interesting to hear Malachi talking about husbands who have 'broken faith' with their wives, and pleading with them to stop and think of the harm being done to the discarded wives.

Malachi is arguing for the kind of responsible living which can never take refuge behind saying, 'It's my own private business' or 'It's quite legal.' Think rather, he says, of the effect of what you are doing on the life of the community as a whole, think above all of its effect on those most deeply and closely involved with you in the situation.

(4) *Ultimate judgement.* Twice Malachi accuses the people of speaking against God. When in their bewilderment they ask 'How?', he is ready with an answer (see Malachi 2:17 and 3:13). You say, he claims, that faith is pointless; it pays no dividends. What evidence is there of a God who judges? 'We for our part count the arrogant happy; it is evildoers who prosper; they have put God to the test

and come to no harm' (Malachi 3:15). Malachi does not deny that there is a problem here, the problem with which we saw Habakkuk wrestling. He counters it by asking people not to be deceived by immediate appearances. Play with fire and you get burnt, sooner or later, burnt with the refining fire of God's judgement.

Malachi depicts such judgement as beginning with the temple and the sudden appearance in it of God's messenger pressing home the demands of the covenant. This passage at the beginning of chapter 3 is probably the one passage in the book familiar to many people. It appears in Handel's 'Messiah', in the famous aria 'But who shall abide the day of his coming.' Many people must have sung it, however, unaware that it comes from Malachi.

From the temple, judgement moves out to embrace all in the community who act to the detriment of their fellow men and women (Malachi 3:5). In the light of the inevitability of such judgement, Malachi is stressing that people are choosing now, by how they live, whether they belong to the faithful who have a future in the purposes of God, or to the wicked who have no such future. But Malachi is no enthusiast for hell-fire and damnation. He believes that the community must be given every opportunity to come into line with God's purposes. That had been one of the main tasks of all the prophets in Israel, to face the people with the need to decide how they would live, to call them to repentance, to do a right about turn. In this context Malachi is the first to mention a belief which was to have a long future, surfacing in the New Testament, for example in Matthew 17:10-11. This was the belief that before the final crisis in the life of the community, the prophet Elijah who, according to 2 Kings 2, had mysteriously disappeared to heaven, would return to earth to heal broken relationships and give the people a last opportunity to prepare for God's coming. In later Jewish celebration of Passover, a place is always set at the table for Elijah, in case he comes.

Behind all that, Malachi says there is the firm conviction that how people live goes hand in hand with what they believe. He looked at a community lacking in enthusiasm, short of moral courage and conviction at all levels, and he knew it was a community with a faulty vision of God. Perhaps the poverty of some of our living is linked to what we really believe, which is often very different from what we say we believe.

ESTHER, A TALE OF LOVE AND HATE

The book of *Esther* has come down to us in two versions: a Hebrew version now in the Old Testament, and a Greek version now in the Apocrypha. There is an excellent translation of the Greek version in the New English Bible Apocrypha. There are many differences between the two, not least the fact that the Greek version makes good an omission which any reader of Esther in the Old Testament soon notices—there are no references to God in the book. Esther 4:15-16, for example, describes how Esther and her maids fasted for three days before seeking an interview with her royal spouse. The Greek version, however, puts on her lips at this point a lengthy prayer in which she pleads with God to demonstrate his power to save his persecuted people. Similarly the Greek version begins with a dream in which Mordecai, who adopted Esther, is forewarned as to what is going to happen, and what God has resolved to do about it.

Introducing God at certain points in the story does not, of course, turn an irreligious book into a religious book, any more than the absence of any reference to God means that the book is of no religious significance. Indeed you can argue that although God is not specifically mentioned in the text of Esther in the Old Testament, nevertheless there runs through the book a strong sense of providence, the hand of God silently at work in all that happens.

Let's test this out by looking at the plot of this historical novel—for that is what it is. It has all the ingredients of a successful novel, beauty and a royal romance, intrigue worthy of Watergate, and suspense sustained to the very end. The setting is the Persian court. In the course of a somewhat drunken party, King Ahasuerus orders his Queen Vashti to appear before his guests to show off her beauty. She refuses. An example has to be made of her, lest other Persian wives follow the royal example of disobeying their husbands. Vashti was banished. A blank in the king's life, however, has to be filled. A 'Miss Persia' beauty contest is organised. The lucky finalists, after a twelve month beauty treatment, have the privilege of spending a night with the king, his favourite to become Queen. A Jewish beauty called Esther gets full marks, and is crowned with due ceremony. How she could have kept Jewish food laws and remained a faithful Jewess as wife of a pagan king, was to worry some Jewish commentators. Meanwhile Mordecai, her adoptive father, keeping a watchful eye on these exciting goings-on, overheard a plot to assassinate the king. A message passed to Esther was instrumental in saving the king's life.

Now the king's favourite adviser was a man called Haman. Mordecai fell foul of him. Haman decided to take his revenge on the minority Jewish community to which Mordecai belonged. With the king's approval a decree is issued throughout the Empire. On a certain day, the 13th day of the month Adar, all Jews, young and old, men, women and children are to be massacred. Esther is in a quandry. She had not revealed her nationality to the king. Nor was she by this time particularly in his favour—she had not seen him for a month! To Mordecai, however, she is the only hope. Taking her courage in both hands, she enters the royal presence unsummoned, normally a capital offence. The king graciously asks what she wants. She requests the pleasure of the company of the king and Haman at a small private party that evening. The evening is an immense success and Esther requests a repeat performance the next evening. Haman, beside himself with joy at such evident signs of royal favour, goes home to supervise the construction of a gallows on which to hang the only fly in the ointment, Mordecai. The king meanwhile, suffering from insomnia, takes to reading some official documents and discovers that nothing had been done to reward the man who had saved his life. Haman, early at the palace next morning to request permission to hang Mordecai, is instead consulted by the king as to a suitable honour for the same man he means to execute. Too late, Haman discovers that the man in question is Mordecai and that Haman personally has to do the honours.

Although it is all very humiliating, there is still the repeat royal dinner party to sweeten the pill. At dinner that evening, Esther reveals her nationality, pleads the cause of her compatriots, and accuses Haman of plotting to exterminate the Jews. Haman ends up on the gallows he had constructed for Mordecai. The king's original decree about the Jews cannot be rescinded, but another decree is hastily issued giving the Jews permission to act in self defence against anyone who attacks them. The fatal day dawns. In the capital Susa, the Jews kill 500 of their enemies. Next day, with special royal permission, they kill another 300. In the provinces, 'they slaughtered seventy-five thousand of those who hated them' (Esther 9:16).

What are we to make of this tale of love and hatred, of persecution and revenge? It is a book which has always caused difficulties. It just got into the Old Testament by the skin of its teeth. Some Jewish teachers were not unnaturally worried lest it rouse the enmity of their gentile neighbours. Self defence has been urged as the sole Jewish motive in this bloody tale; but self defence can hardly explain how a minority group is supposed to have killed over 75,000 Persians in the Persian Empire. Paradoxically, a copy of Esther is the prize possession of many Jewish families and it is the only book in the Old Testament which can be read in the synagogue in any language. Its popularity is linked with the celebration of the festival of *Purim*. According to the story, it was the events of the 13th and 14th of Adar which gave birth to the festival of Purim. The word 'Purim' meaning 'lots', is supposed to derive from an incident in the story when Haman casts lots to decide the precise date of the massacre of the Jews. Purim, in spite of the fact that it is the only festival in the Jewish calendar which cannot claim the authority of Moses, has become one of the most popular festivals in the Jewish liturgical year. It is celebrated joyously in a carnival atmosphere, with, in modern Israel, processions through the streets and floats bearing effigies of all the leading characters in the story. If we ask, 'why it's popularity?', the answer is that it speaks to something deep-seated in the life and needs of the community, as all true celebration must.

The story, and hence the festival, come out of a situation in the second century BC when there was increasing friction between Jewish minority groups and the communities in which they had settled. The Jews were different; and to be different is to provoke suspicion, misunderstanding, hatred and, all too often, violence. This has sadly been a recurring experience for the Jews, not least in so-called Christian countries, not least at the instigation of the Church. It has written one of the most appalling chapters in the history of the twentieth century—Auschwitz, Belsen, Buchenwald, the ghetto and the gas chamber—and in the midst of it all the stubborn miracle of Jewish survival. It is this miracle which the festival of Purim celebrates. In the celebration the Jewish community expresses and holds on to its identity, an identity which it believes comes from God. The book of Esther has never been merely a historical novel for the Jewish people; it has been too near the bitter edge of their experience for that. It takes a Jewish girl and makes her Queen of Persia so that in the hour of crisis she may listen to the words '... who knows whether it is not for a time like this that you have become queen?' (Esther 4:14). Providence can work in strange and unexpected ways.

If you are appalled by the words of bitterness and the deeds of bloody revenge in the story, so be it—so am I! It is all too easy for people to confuse their own raw emotions, prejudices and hatred, with the will of God. Our own world is full of examples, from Northern Ireland to Lebanon, from South Africa to Israel. We can never know how we might react if we were brought to the bitter edge of the experience which is enshrined in the book of Esther.

DANIEL, LIVING WITH HOPE

As the lights are lit in Christian homes to celebrate Christmas, so in Jewish homes the lights are lit to celebrate the festival of *Hanukkah*. Hanukkah recalls the events of a December day in 164 BC when, after three years of bitter guerrilla warfare, Jewish patriots drove foreign occupation troops from most of Jerusalem; and the temple, which had been defiled by the symbols of a pagan religion, was cleansed and re-consecrated to the worship of the God of Israel (see p 27). It was sometime during these three years that one of the Jewish freedom fighters, a man of deep religious convictions, penned the book of *Daniel*. It is the manifesto of a resistance movement, which was prepared to face death in defence of its faith.

(1) *How to misunderstand.* Settle down into a comfortable armchair, put your feet up, think yourself into the mood to tackle a difficult biblical crossword puzzle, and you can have a marvellous time with the book of Daniel. There are strange and puzzling clues scattered all over the place. There are visions of a giant statue, made of gold, silver, iron and clay, being shattered by a stone (Daniel 2:31ff); of a towering tree cut down till only a stump is left in the ground (Daniel 4); of four strange beasts rising out of the sea (Daniel 7); of the ram and the he-goat, of horns and a little horn (Daniel 8). The interpretation of the detail in some of these visions leaves plenty of scope for the imagination. Then there is the mysterious writing on the wall (Daniel 5).

If, on the other hand, you have a fondness for playing with numbers, there are plenty of them around—sevens and seventy times seven, 1150 days, 1290 days and 1335 days. In such respects, the book is an example of a type of literature which we call 'Apocalyptic', from a Greek word meaning 'unveiling', unveiling the still unknown future. The New Testament contains one example of this in the book of Revelation. We know of many others which never got into the Bible. Just because so much of what apocalyptic books have to say comes in mysterious and cryptic form, such books have become the happy hunting ground for religious enthusiasts and cranks throughout the ages. If you want to find references in the Bible to the communist threat to western civilisation, or to the Arab–Israeli conflict, or uncomplimentary references to the Pope or any rival religious sect which you regard as heretical, this is where you look. If you want to calculate the date of the end of the world, it is here, easily discovered if only you find the right system. Don't let the fact that other people have miscalculated the date of the end of the world from fool-proof references in the book of Daniel discourage you. Obviously, they had just got the wrong system.

135

From the comfortable depths of that armchair, a fertile and pious imagination will enable you to spend many a happy hour wholly misunderstanding the book of Daniel. You would do better to let your thoughts take to the hills to join the freedom fighters, to live with people for whom the penalty for possessing a copy of their sacred scripture was death. If you are prepared to ask how people can live with hope in a world where ruthless and arrogant power seems to triumph, where evil seems unchallengingly strong and goodness pitifully weak, then take another look at the book of Daniel.

(2) *Stories of Faith.* The book falls into two main sections. Chapters 1-6 contain, in the main, stories about a loyal Jew called Daniel and some companions, who lived in exile in Babylon during the sixth century BC. Many stories about Daniel seem to have circulated within the Jewish community. You will find others in some of the books that didn't get into our Bible. The author of our book took some of these stories and used them for his own purposes. His knowledge of the sixth century BC is pretty hazy and confused, but the portraits he draws of Daniel and his friends are vivid and clear.

All of them, particularly Daniel, rise to positions of influence at the Babylonian court, but never at the cost of compromising their religious convictions. To avoid breaking Jewish food regulations, they live as vegetarians at the Babylonian court, the result being that they are healthier and stronger than others at court (Daniel 1:8-16). This is not intended as an argument for vegetarianism; it is proof of the providence of God.

Shadrach, Meschach and Abednego refuse to worship the golden statue erected by the Emperor. They are fully aware of the consequences. They face them with unflinching courage and faith: 'If there is a god who is able to save us from the blazing furnace, it is our God whom we serve; he will deliver us from your majesty's power. But if not, be it known to your majesty that we shall neither serve your gods nor worship the gold image you have set up' (Daniel 3:17-18). Similarly Daniel continues his own religious practices in defiance of a royal decree and ends up in a lions' den. In both cases the stories tell of miraculous interventions. God delivers; but Daniel and his friends are prepared to die for their beliefs. It is a faith which draws strength from the conviction that the God of Israel alone knows and determines what happens in life. Babylonian astrologers, wizards and magicians are powerless to describe or to interpret troubling royal dreams. Not so Daniel; as the servant of this all-knowing God he possesses such power.

(3) *Visions of Faith*. In the second section of the book, chapters 7-12, Daniel, instead of being a skilled interpreter of dreams, receives a series of visions which have to be explained to him by angelic interpreters. All the visions are said to have been given to Daniel in the sixth century BC, and are supposed to describe events lying in the still unknown future for someone living then. In fact this is not so. The author is writing in the 60s of the second century BC. He uses the visions to trace in broad outline what is to him past history from the sixth century onwards, his information becoming more and more detailed as he approaches the events of his own day. He then claims to unveil what still lies in the future.

It is impossible to discuss the details of these visions briefly. Indeed some of the detail is still far from clear. It is, in any case, far more important to see what lies behind the visions. They are shot through with the conviction that human history is meaningful, and that whatever appearances there may be to the contrary, it is God's meaning and God's purposes which are being worked out, even in and through the diabolical evil of people. Past, present and future lie in God's sure hands. If in faith we confess 'In the beginning God', so must we declare 'In the end God.' Whatever megalomaniac rulers or power-crazed politicians may believe, history is moving towards a goal, God's goal which can only be known by his people. No evil, not even death itself can thwart God's purposes. So we hear in the book of Daniel of the dead rising, some to share in the everlasting joy of God's coming kingdom, and others who have opposed God's purposes in this world, to face God's judgement (Daniel 12:1-3). It is interesting that this hope, one of the earliest expressions of life hereafter in the Bible, arises solely from the conviction that it is God who must have the last word on human life and destiny.

(4) *God alone is King*. It is important to realise that these visions are not intended to encourage people to peer into the unknown future or to calculate the day and the hour of the end of human history. They are a call to people to live courageously in the here and now. 'Do not be afraid, men greatly beloved,' says an angelic interpreter to Daniel, 'all will be well with you. Take heart, and be strong.' (Daniel 10:19). Both sections of the book therefore serve the same purpose. Over against all human totalitarianism, they place the unchallengeable supremacy of God. Here is the witness of people who will accept no absolute but God. They may be crushed by human juggernauts, but never broken. They are prepared to live and, if necessary, to die defiantly and with hope. If there have to be martyrs, then the book of Daniel provides a faith for martyrs. It bears witness to unshakeable convictions which can put iron into weak souls:

> ... for he is the living God, the everlasting,
>   whose kingly power will never be destroyed;
>   whose sovereignty will have no end—
> a saviour, a deliverer, a worker of signs and wonders,
>   in heaven and on earth ...

(Daniel 6:26-27)

6

People and Book

Before looking at the shape of the Old Testament as a whole and then more closely at some books within it, we took a brief journey through the history of the people of Israel. That journey was necessary because it took us into a world very different from our own, the world in which the people of Israel lived. We had to take that journey because we cannot hope to understand the book apart from the people whose experience it enshrines. Whatever views we may hold about the authority or inspiration of the Bible, the Old Testament did not suddenly drop one day from heaven, neatly packaged in divine wrapping paper. We have seen how it grew round a central core, TORAH, the Law, and gathered to itself across many years a rich variety of material. But why did certain books come together to form the Old Testament, while other books, which we know of, did not?

It is a complicated story, but there is little doubt that the books which survived did so because they had the ability to continue to speak to the needs of the people. They provided direction for daily living; they helped to keep faith alive in difficult times and they gave people courage to face the ever changing demands of life. So out of the experience of the people came the book, and the book continued to nourish the people.

To understand what the books of the Old Testament have to say to us, we must first learn to look at them against their background in the life of ancient Israel. Very often we can only truly tune in to what is being said to and through a prophet if we know something of the social, political and religious factors at work in his day. True, all the different books have come together to form one collection, and each has something to contribute to the whole, but we miss a lot unless we first listen to each book in its own setting in the life of Israel.

I was standing one day beside a small Highland burn. It was winding its way down the hillside, soon to flow like many another burn into the River Dee. I knew it would end up making its contribution to the deeper, surging waters of the Dee, and the Dee in turn would flow into the sea. That was where it was heading; that was its importance, the contribution it would make, along with others, to a larger river. Yet as I listened to that burn as it chuckled its way over stones or rushed defiantly through a narrow gorge, it had its own character and was making its own sounds, sounds which would be lost when it joined the Dee. If I had not been prepared to stand there and listen, I would have missed something. So is it with every book in the Old Testament, and sometimes with different parts within the one book. They are all going to make their contribution to the Old Testament, but each has its distinctive character and message which we shall hear only if we are prepared to listen to it against its own background in the landscape of ancient Israel. It is worth making the effort to listen.

DIFFERENT BACKGROUNDS

Here is one example of the way in which our knowledge of the particular circumstances in which a part of the Old Testament is written can help us to understand what it has to say. Apart from questions of literacy style, there are very good reasons for believing that Isaiah 40-55 were not written by Isaiah of Jerusalem who lived in Jerusalem towards the end of the eighth century BC. In Isaiah's day the foreign power central to the crisis in Judah's political life was Assyria, the 'rod of God's anger' as it is described in Isaiah 10:5. In Isaiah 40-55 there is no longer any mention of Assyria; the foreign power centre stage is Babylon, which only came to the fore when the Assyrian Empire collapsed in the last quarter of the seventh century BC. The message of Isaiah 40-55 is essentially one of encouragement, of helping people to pick up the broken fragments of their faith. What had shattered that faith was the destruction of Jerusalem, that supposedly indestructible city of God, in 587 BC, and the subsequent exile of many Jews to Babylon. Prior to the destruction of Jerusalem, most of the prophets have at the centre of their message a word of judgement against a complacent and corrupt community. Isaiah of Jerusalem is no exception. He has some harsh words to say:

Woe betide those who add house to house and join field to field,
   until everyone else is displaced ...

Woe betide those who drag wickedness and sin along,
   as with a sheep's tether or a heifer's rope ...

Woe betide those who call evil good and good evil,
   who make darkness light and light darkness,
   who make bitter sweet and sweet bitter.
Woe betide those who are wise in their own sight
   and prudent in their own esteem.
Woe betide those heroic topers, those valiant mixers of drink,
   who for a bribe acquit the guilty
      and deny justice to those in the right.
                                                      (Isaiah 5:8,18,20-23).

To such a people the cutting edge of the true prophet's message cannot be one of comfort. You don't preach judgement, however, to a broken people who have passed through the fire of judgement. Then is the time to rebuild on the foundation of the steadfast grace of God and to challenge the people to let that grace reshape their lives. That is the central message of Isaiah 40-55. It makes sense, it is a relevant word to the people in exile coping with the problems in the middle of the sixth century BC. It does not make sense, it is not a relevant word in the age of Isaiah of Jerusalem 150 years earlier. It is a measure of the greatness of the anonymous poet of Isaiah 40-55 that, knowing the teaching of Isaiah of Jerusalem as he certainly did, he took it and adapted it to meet the needs of his own day. God does not speak in a social, political or spiritual vacuum. To understand the word as it came to people *then*, we must know something of the circumstances in which it was spoken.

DIFFERENT VOICES

It is not, however, only different historical situations that lead us to hear different voices in the books of the Old Testament. The Old Testament is an uncomfortable book for anyone who wishes to claim that there is only one genuine type of religious experience—their own, of course—and only one correct way of talking about God. On the contrary, the Old Testament introduces us to a rich variety of religious experience and many different ways of describing it. As we have seen (see pp 51f) the prophetic books are full of phrases like, 'the word of the LORD came to me' or 'thus says the LORD' (*eg* Jeremiah 1:4,11,13; 2:5). They are claiming the authority of a personal encounter with God. Many of the prophets also describe visions, sometimes visions which have at their centre something quite ordinary, like an almond tree bursting into blossom or a boiling pot (Jeremiah 1:11-14), sometimes visions with weird and extraordinary features (see Ezekiel 1).

Other Old Testament books, however, make no such claim in terms of 'the word of God', and recount no such visions. That is true of the teaching of the 'wise men' in Israel, as you find it in the book of Proverbs. It is based on shrewd observation of human experience and human nature. All that Proverbs in its present form claims is that the wise and good life is based upon 'the fear of the LORD' (*eg* Proverbs 1:7). Or take the book of Ecclesiastes. It makes no appeal to any word from the LORD. It is full of a man's intensely personal reflections on life ... 'I said to myself' ... 'I saw' ... 'I applied my mind' ... and very strange reflections they are, when you set them against much that you find elsewhere in the Old Testament.

Perhaps the best illustration of what I mean is to be found in one book, the book of Genesis. In the stories about the patriarchs, Abraham, Isaac and Jacob, there is a clear pattern. God is repeatedly introduced as speaking directly to them: 'The LORD said to Abraham, 'Leave your own country ...' (Genesis 12:1); 'The LORD appeared to

Isaac and said, 'Do not go down to Egypt ...' (Genesis 26:2). Often this speaking comes to these people at certain well-known sacred sites: to Abraham, for example, at 'the sanctuary at Shechem, the terebinth tree of Moreh' (Genesis 12:6); to Jacob 'at a certain shrine' called Bethel (Genesis 28:11ff). You might think that such a picture of the way in which God communicates with people would continue right through Genesis, but it doesn't. When we come to the stories about Joseph in chapters 37ff, we enter a different world. There are no references to God speaking to Joseph, nor any appearances at sacred sites. Yet the Joseph story is still the story of the out-working of God's providence. At the end, Joseph says to the brothers who had sold him into slavery: 'You meant to do me harm; but God meant to bring good out of it ...' (Genesis 50:20). This is just as much a story of God at work, as are the stories that centre on Abraham, Isaac and Jacob, but it is told in a very different way. That is as it should be. There is no one way of talking about God in the Old Testament, any more than there is one way of talking about God today, even among those of us who call ourselves Christian.

Personally I find myself relating much more easily to the Joseph story. If the words 'The LORD spoke to Abraham' means that Abraham clearly heard the voice of God speaking to him from heaven, then I have never had such an experience. Nor would I claim to have seen visions in which God has appeared to me. I do believe, however, that I can look back across my life at various moments, which seemed puzzling and not easily understood at the time, and say *'but God.'* I am convinced there has been, and is, a divine purpose running through life, even when I fail to recognise it.

It is hardly surprising that, in a collection of books which come to us from many centuries in the life of a people and from many different experiences, there should be such richness and variety. Tune into it, even when some of its notes seem strange and harsh to you. Only once you have tried to listen to what it sounded like *then* in the world of the Old Testament, will you be in a position responsibly to ask what it may mean *now* for us today.

What then does it, or can it say to us today? We don't live in the world of the Old Testament. We are not ancient Israelites; we are not even Jews. There is no use pretending that the Old Testament is for Christians an easy book. It has never been. Indeed, looking back across the history of the church, I am tempted to say that the Old Testament has ceased to be a problem for Christians only when it has been misunderstood, when Christians have tried to read into it all kinds of things which are not really there. Too often Christians have used the Old Testament simply as a book in which to find hidden references to Jesus. The number you find will depend almost entirely upon your imagination and your ingenuity. It has always been more tempting, indeed easier to do this, than to listen to what the Old Testament is actually saying. This is not to deny that Christians can justifiably claim that the pilgrimage and faith of ancient Israel find their fulfilment in Jesus. That should not, however, be taken as an invitation to ransack the Old Testament to find in it hidden clues to Jesus. Rather it gives us a particular vantage point from which we can look back and see how certain things in the Old Testament lead only to dead ends, while others will throb with life. When you are travelling it is important to know what the dead ends are. Nor do all the roads in the Old Testament lead to Jesus or the Christian faith. Some lead far more easily to Judaism.

But shouldn't the way in which the New Testament writers handle the Old Testament be our guide here, if we claim to be Christian? Yes indeed, yes … and no. No, because the writers of the New Testament were children of their own age, most of them first century Jews using the kind of arguments which would be understandable and convincing to thoughtful people in their own day, but are no longer necessarily so for us who are not first century Jews.

We have already looked at one or two examples of this (see p xi). Let us take another. In Galatians 3:16ff Paul talks of God's promises having been given to Abraham and to his 'seed' (eg Genesis 12:7). He makes a great deal of the fact that the word translated 'seed' is singular. Therefore the promises point forward not to many people, but to one person, namely Jesus. Now this is the kind of argument which could be used and understood by any Jewish Rabbi in Paul's day, but how convincing is it to us? The word 'seed' is a collective noun. It is no more simply singular, pointing to one person, than our word 'people.' Most modern versions of the Bible quite correctly translate it by the plural 'descendants' at Genesis 12:7. To this extent we have to say 'no' to Paul's argument. But don't let us throw out the baby with the bath water. This is only one of many ways in which, in terms understandable to his own day, Paul expresses his conviction that the story of God and Israel comes to its climax in Jesus. The challenge facing us as Christians today is to discover ways in which we can still say this, and say it as convincingly as Paul did in his own day.

One thing above all seems clear to me at this point. There is no short cut. *We must first listen to what the Old Testament has to say for itself.* Sadly, few Christians are prepared to do this. For most people within the church, much of the Old Testament is untrodden terrain, a country which many have no desire to visit since its inhabitants are thought to be strange, barbaric and unfriendly. There is nothing much of interest to be seen apart from a few well-known landmarks, such as the Ten Commandments and some of the Psalms. I hope I have encouraged you to consider making a journey into that untrodden terrain. Wherever you go you will need a guide. The *Daily Study Bible* series (Saint Andrew Press) is as good as any.

Sometimes the going will be rough. Don't be put off when you find yourself having to say, 'I don't understand this' or 'In the light of what I know about Jesus, this can't be true.' Travel on. Again and again you will find yourself drawn up sharply in your travels, sometimes faced by a vision of God which will haunt you and lead you to ask questions about yourself and the world in which you live. Sometimes you will be disturbed and challenged by words which cut through the cocoon of social and religious pretence in which we so often wrap ourselves. Don't go around hunting for souvenirs to take back to your Christian home with you. Far more important than the souvenirs is what will be happening to you along the journey. You will find your horizons widened, your prejudices questioned, your mind and heart enriched. That at least has been the experience of many who have travelled this way before you. It certainly has been mine. The further you travel the more you will find yourself saying: 'Isn't there something curiously familiar about what is going on here?' You are liable to come across fellow-travellers whose experience of faith and discipleship joins hands with yours.

Here is a man saying to his people in the name of God:

Your loyalty to me is like the morning mist,
    like dew that vanishes early.   (Hosea 6:4)

Then you remember the vows you have taken and seldom truly kept, the promises you have made to God and broken, the enthusiasms you have had which have died away, your repeated failures. But you also hear the same man talking about God's loyalty, about God's love for Israel which is strangely unlike Israel's love, because it is undeserved, strong, steadfast—and nothing, not even Israel's failures, can break or stop it (Hosea 11:9). It is then you are reminded that your faith rests not in your grasp of God—it wouldn't last long if it did—but in God's grasp of you.

Here are two men clashing in the temple of Jerusalem in an age of crisis. Each of them with passionate sincerity proclaims, 'Thus says the LORD', and each delivers a message which directly contradicts that of the other (see Jeremiah 28). Who is right? What were ordinary folk listening to this clash, to make of it? How could they be sure what God's will was? We still listen to contradictory voices within the church on some of the major issues of our day. Should we as Christians be committed to the Campaign for Nuclear Disarmament, or is there a case to be argued for the nuclear deterrent. What of abortion? Is it always wrong or are their circumstances in which it is justifiable as the lesser of two evils? In debates among Christians we hear voices with passionate sincerity claiming, on both sides, that their view is a reflection of the will of God in our time. There were no easy or self-evident answers for many people in Jerusalem in Jeremiah's day. On many issues, there are none today which can claim without fear of contradiction, 'Thus says the LORD.'

Here are voices triumphantly affirming that the world in which they live is God's world, God's creation, a vast yet good world of mystery and wonder (*eg* Genesis 1; Psalm 8); voices that dare to say that in the midst of all the turmoil and changes of human history, it is God's will that is being worked out in ways we often fail to see, and that it is God's purpose which must ultimately triumph. Don't we desperately need to hear such voices today as we begin to understand the ecological crisis we face and tremble on the brink of possible nuclear holocaust?

Here are voices, agonised voices struggling to make sense of a world that seems to have gone mad, a world of injustice and cruelty, a world apparently meaningless. They are agonised voices precisely because they can neither turn a blind eye to God, nor can they deny the dark side of their experience. They refuse to accept the slick and easy answers, even when they are handed out to them by the religion of their day. Often they find themselves having to settle for something less than certainty (*eg* Job, Ecclesiastes and some of the Psalms). If we have never found ourselves struggling with similar perplexities and unanswered or half-answered questions today, I wonder whether we are being honest?

Here are voices .... We could go on multiplying examples, but if you are not convinced by this time that it is at least worth considering a journey into the strange world of the Old Testament, a few more examples will hardly make any difference.

There is a rich and varied country here waiting to be explored, a country whose secrets only reveal themselves to those who traverse it with an open mind and a healthy dose of curiosity. At every turn you will find the God from whose presence you can never escape, the God who is there in the darkness as surely as in the light, the God who in the fulness of time came into the world he created as the Father of our Lord Jesus Christ. You will also discover the Old Testament story and the experience of Israel continuing in those who, in and through Jesus, find themselves to be the descendants of Abraham. Bon voyage!

For Further Reading

In addition to the Saint Andrew Press *Daily Study Bible* series (Old and New Testament), there are useful brief commentaries on every book in the Old Testament in the Tyndale *Bible Commentaries* and in the Cambridge *New English Bible* series.

If you wish to brush away Old Testament cobwebs, as useful a way of doing it as any is to dip into Alan T Dale, *Winding Quest, the Heart of the Old Testament in Plain English*. Etienne Charpentier, *How to Read the Old Testament* provides a brief, but stimulating introduction into some of the problems of reading the Old Testament. For those who wish to go further, B W Anderson, *The Living World of the Old Testament* (fourth edition) is good value.

It is worth investing in a one volume Bible Dictionary, such as the Harper *Bible Dictionary* or the *Interpreter's Dictionary of the Bible*. On a more modest, but attractive scale, there is the Lion *Concise Bible Handbook*.

About the Author

ROBERT DAVIDSON MA, BD, DD, FRSE was born in Fife, Scotland and educated at the University of St Andrews. He lectured at Aberdeen, St Andrews and Edinburgh Universities before becoming Professor of Biblical Studies at the University of Glasgow. He was Moderator of the General Assembly of the Church of Scotland in 1990 and currently serves as the Interim General Secretary of the Department of Education of the Church of Scotland.